HISTORY
IN CLOSE-UP

THE AGE OF DISCOVERY

COLOURPOINT
EDUCATIONAL

Audrey M Hodge

First Edition
Third Impression, 2015

ISBN: 978 1 906578 43 5

Published by: Colourpoint Educational
Layout and design: April Sky Design
Printed by: W&G Baird Ltd, Antrim

About The Authors

Audrey Hodge is a Senior Teacher at Omagh Academy, Co Tyrone. She obtained her MA in Modern and Contemporary History at the University of Ulster. She is co-author of *Union to Partition* (Colourpoint 1995) and of *The Race to Rule's* fore-runner, *Britain, Ireland and Europe from 1570–1745*. She has also written *Gallows and Turnkeys* which is a short history of Omagh Gaol, and *A Congregation in the Omey* (1997) which is a history of First Omagh Presbyterian Church.

This edition has been updated with additional input from Sheila Johnston, Hazel Caldwell and Wesley Johnston.

COLOURPOINT
EDUCATIONAL

Colourpoint Educational
An imprint of Colourpoint Creative Ltd
Colourpoint House
Jubilee Business Park
Jubilee Road
Newtownards
County Down
Northern Ireland
BT23 4YH

Tel: 028 9182 6339
Fax: 028 9182 1900
E-mail: sales@colourpoint.co.uk
Web site: www.colourpointeducational.com

CONTENTS

ICONS USED IN THIS BOOK

GUIDE TO ICONS

 ACTIVITY

 BEFORE YOU START

 BY THE WAY

 PROJECT

 RESEARCH

 REVIEW

 TIP

 WORD BOX

 WRITER INFO

 QUESTIONS

SKILLS AND CAPABILITIES KEY

 COMMUNICATION

 MATHS

 USING ICT

 MANAGING INFORMATION

 THINKING, PROBLEM SOLVING, DECISION MAKING

 BEING CREATIVE

 WORKING WITH OTHERS

 SELF MANAGEMENT

The period from the first Tudor monarch, Henry VII in 1485, until the arrival of a Hanoverian monarch, George I in 1714, witnessed great changes in Britain.

Many famous events took place also at this time. Henry VIII had six wives, Mary Queen of Scots was beheaded, the Spanish Armada was defeated, and the English Civil War and the famous battles at the Boyne and Aughrim took place.

This is therefore a period full of romance, intrigue and adventure. The map below shows what Europe looked like in 1570. The Holy Roman Empire was a loose federation of independent states.

> **TUDOR, HANOVERIAN:** the names of two families who were the Kings and Queens of England at different times.

Europe in 1570

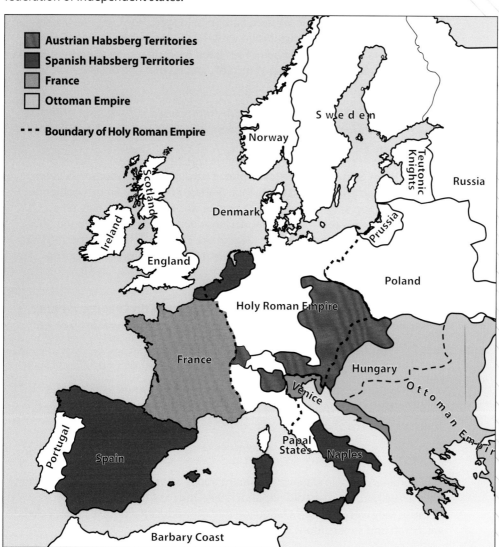

Compare this map to a modern map of Europe. How has it changed? What countries still exist today? Which ones do not?

A lot happened during the period covered by this book. **Pirates** became common in the 1500s. In a later unit you will study a famous pirate called **Drake**. Write down everything you know about pirates. What did they do? Why did they do this? Where did they sail? What did they look like? Who did they meet? Keep your notes safe so that you can look at them again at the end of this section.

THE STATE OF THE CHURCH

Until the early sixteenth century the Roman Catholic church was the church to which Christian people in western Europe belonged. However, many were beginning to become very dissatisfied with the church and its leaders. Some Popes (leaders of the church) had not set good examples, such as Rodrigo Borgia who was elected Pope Alexander VI in 1492. This is what one observer wrote about his election:

> *Borgia openly bribed many of the cardinals, some with money, others with promises of profitable jobs, of which he had many at that time in his power.*

Another Pope, Sextus IV, made his nephews cardinals. The bishops, too, were often poor examples of good behaviour. Jean de Lorainne, a French nobleman, became a bishop at the age of three. Later he was made bishop over nine more dioceses and abbot of nine monasteries. King Ferdinand of Aragon got appointments in the church for his illegitimate children. It is not surprising then that some ordinary priests and monks were not good examples either. The following sources tell us more.

> *A monk there was, one of the finest sort who rode the country; hunting was his sport ... Hunting a hare or riding at a fence was all his fun, he spared for no expense.*
>
> From the *Canterbury Tales* by Geoffrey Chaucer.
>
> *They lack all education. They understand nothing at all of what they sing. The holy scriptures are never seen in their hands. They never discuss or preach and they take no account of training in morals.*
>
> A German monk writing about other monks in 1493.

Many ordinary people were very ignorant about what the church and Christianity were actually about. They did not understand much of their church services because they were in Latin, a language that only educated people knew. Beliefs in witchcraft and superstitions were widespread.

THE REFORMERS

People who wished to change or reform the church were known as Reformers. Some of these were **Sir Thomas More**, **Erasmus** of Rotterdam, **Girolamo Savonarola** and, the best known, **Martin Luther**.

Martin Luther was born in Eisleben (in Saxony, now part of Germany) in **1483**.

BISHOP: An official in charge of a diocese

DIOCESE: The church in a particular region.

CARDINAL: A senior bishop.

When he was 17 he went to the University of Erfurt and during his time there he decided to become a monk. He lived a very strict life, but was not really happy.

Luther became particularly angry over the church's sale of indulgences to help raise money to rebuild St Peter's Cathedral in Rome. Buying an 'indulgence' from the church meant you could spend less time suffering in Purgatory after you died.

This is what Martin Luther later said about his time as a monk:

> *I would have become a martyr through fasting, prayer, reading and other good works had I remained a monk much longer.*

Explain, in your own words, what an indulgence was. Why do you think Martin Luther might have objected to the church selling indulgences?

Luther became convinced that the church needed to changed. In 1517 Luther nailed a list of 95 points which he wished to have discussed to the door of Wittenberg church. These were known as the **95 Theses**. His outspoken ideas made many church leaders, including the Pope, very angry. The Pope wrote to Luther demanding that he retract these criticisms or be excommunicated. In 1520 Luther burned the Pope's letter. A student witnessed the event and wrote:

> *The next day Dr Luther warned us that it was easy to burn the Pope's letter and books. But we needed to end completely the rule of the Pope. Dr Luther said it would be better to live lonely in a desert than under the laws of the Pope.*

Martin Luther burning the Pope's letter.

Luther read the Bible carefully and he also wrote several pamphlets which were read eagerly by many. In fact Luther became a sort of hero to many Germans.

The picture above was drawn in the eighteenth century. What impression of Martin Luther is the artist trying to put across here? How has he done this? What adjectives would you use to describe the emotions in this picture?

ACTIVITY

Look at this painting of Martin Luther. It was painted by Noel Paton in 1861. Discuss the painting in your class. What is happening in the picture? What book do you think he is reading? Do you think the painter is sympathetic to Martin Luther? Why or why not? What do you think is the significance of the figure shown under the table? Can you see a skull? What do you think the artist means by including it?

Luther was summoned by the Holy Roman Emperor to a special court called the **Diet** at **Worms** in **1521**. Luther defended his actions:

> *An immense crowd greeted the appearance of the arch-heretic who was questioned before the Emperor and the Princes.*
>
> *Luther said "I stand convinced by the scriptures I have studied. I cannot and will not take back anything, for to act against my conscience is neither safe nor honest."*
>
> Cardinal Alexander

The Emperor Charles V ordered Luther to go home and stop his preaching, which he did. Luther was afraid for his safety, and was offered protection by Prince Frederick, a sympathetic nobleman from Luther's home region of Saxony. During this time Luther began to translate the New Testament into German as well as writing some hymns. For almost a year, he stayed away from any open controversy. Nevertheless, more and more people came to agree with him.

His followers were known as **Lutherans** or **Protestants** because they protested against the teachings of the Roman Catholic Church. This great change, or **Reformation**, spread from Germany across Europe and eventually all over the world during the sixteenth century.

Martin Luther married a former nun, Catherine von Bora, in 1525 and they had six children (three sons and three daughters). He died in 1546.

Construct a time line for the life of Martin Luther, using these dates:
1483, 1500, 1517, 1520, 1521, 1525, 1546.

ACTIVITY

Study all the sources in this Unit. With a partner, select the criticisms which could be levelled at the church. Do you think they were justified? Explain your answer.

ACTIVITY

Hot Seat

Pick two people to sit at the front, facing the class. One will play the part of Martin Luther and the other will play the part of Emperor Charles V.

The rest of the class can ask them questions and they must answer them. Think up your own questions but here are two examples of what you might ask:

"Martin Luther, aren't you going too far by telling people to reject the Pope?"

"Charles, why do you want Martin Luther to stop preaching?"

UNIT 3: THE ENGLISH REFORMATION

HENRY VIII

King Henry VIII ruled England from 1509 until 1547. He was a loyal Catholic and was shocked by Luther's teachings. He believed the Pope was the head of the Church: indeed the Pope had given him the title '*Fidei Defensor*', (Defender of the Faith) because Henry had written a book criticising Luther.

Despite this, Henry was the King who was responsible for England breaking away from the church in Rome. Henry's motives were more political than religious: it was Henry's son Edward VI who was to be responsible for the real introduction of Protestantism to England, as we will see in the next unit. In 1527 Henry decided to divorce his wife Catherine of Aragon, to whom he had been married for 18 years.

WHY DID HENRY WANT A DIVORCE?

There are various reasons why Henry wanted a divorce. He was desperate for a son to be heir to the throne. He had also met and become infatuated with one of Catherine's young maids, called Anne Boleyn. In addition, he had also found a passage in the Bible that troubled him because of his strong belief in the teachings of the church. Read these sources:

> "Good wife though she was, Catherine of Aragon had failed in her primary function, to provide Henry with a healthy male heir. It had not been for lack of trying. She had borne her first baby in January 1510. It had been a daughter, still-born. Within a year she produced a son... but then the child had sickened and died. 1513 saw the birth of another boy, and 1514 yet another, but neither survived. In the same year Catherine was delivered prematurely of a fourth son, still-born. Not until 1516 did she produce a sturdy child, and then it was a girl, christened Mary. There were several more pregnancies, but no son came, and before long Catherine's pregnancies ceased."
>
> *The Life and Times of King Henry VIII*, Robert Lacy, 1972

> "The King had tired of his wife and fallen in love with Anne Boleyn, who would give herself entirely to him only if he would give himself entirely to her".
>
> *Henry VIII*, Jack Scarisbrick, 1968

> "And if a man shall take his brother's wife, it is an unclean thing: ... they shall be childless."
>
> *The Bible*, Leviticus 20:21 (Catherine of Aragon had previously been married to Henry's elder brother Arthur, who had died.)

The British monarch still holds the title "Defender of the Faith" today, and the letters 'FD' still appear on coins in the United Kingdom. Queen Elizabeth II's full title is "Elizabeth the Second, by the Grace of God, of the United Kingdom of Great Britain and Northern Ireland and of Her other Realms and Territories Queen, Head of the Commonwealth, Defender of the Faith".

Catherine of Aragon

Anne Boleyn

What does each source state were the reasons for Henry wanting a divorce? Which reason do you think was the most important? Why do you think this?

Henry VIII

> **EXCOMMUNICATE:** To sever all links between a person and the church.

Roman numerals are an old way of writing numbers:

I = 1   II = 2   III = 3
IV = 4   V = 5   VI = 6
VII = 7   VIII = 8   IX = 9

They are often used in the titles of kings and queens.

THE BREAK WITH ROME

The only person who could grant Henry his divorce was the Head of the Church, and that was the Pope. He, of course, refused permission since divorce was against Church law and also because Catherine was the Aunt of Charles V, a very powerful man in Europe at that time and with whom the Pope was living.

Henry was not pleased, so in response he decided to break the link with Rome by making himself head of the Church in England. To do this, Henry formed the Reformation Parliament in 1529 which passed laws limiting the power of Rome. The Pope responded by excommunicating Henry.

In 1533 the Archbishop of Canterbury, Thomas Cranmer, granted Henry his divorce and married Henry and Anne Boleyn, who was pregnant at that time. Henry then refused to pay any more money to the Pope and had Parliament pass the **Act of Supremacy** 1534. This declared that the King was the Head of the Church in England.

Catherine died in 1536. Henry went on to marry a total of six times before his death in 1547, as shown in this table:

NAME OF WIFE	DATES MARRIED TO HENRY	CHILDREN	HOW THE MARRIAGE ENDED
Catherine of Aragon	1509 – 1533	One daughter, Mary	Divorce
Anne Boleyn	1533 – 1536	One daughter, Elizabeth	Execution
Jane Seymour	1536 –1537	One son, Edward	Death in childbirth
Anne of Cleves	Jan–July 1540	None	Divorced
Kathryn Howard	1540 – 1542	None	Executed
Katherine Parr	1542 – 1547	None	Widowed

Q Both Henry VIII and Martin Luther broke the link with Rome. Were their motives similar or different? Explain your answer.

RESEARCH

Choose one of Henry VIII's last four wives, and find out as much as you can about them. Where were they born? Who were their parents? Why did Henry marry them? How did the marriage end, and why? What do you learn about Henry from the experiences of his six wives?

Despite his desperation for an heir, none of Henry's three children had any children of their own, so after they had all died the throne eventually passed to the Scottish Stuart family because Henry's sister Margaret Tudor had married the Stuart king of Scotland. The family tree on the opposite page shows the royal family tree from the time of Henry VIII's father until the early eighteenth century. The dates given are the years that each person was the king or queen. You will meet many of these monarchs in the rest of this book but first we will study the reigns of each of Henry VIII's three children.

Tudors

Stuarts

Henry VII (1485–1509)

Henry VIII (1509–1547)

Margaret Tudor
m James IV (1488–1513) of Scotland

Edward VI
(1547–1553)

Mary I
(1553–1558)
no children

Elizabeth I
(1558–1603)
no children

Margaret

James V (1513–1542) of Scotland

Henry Stuart
(Lord Darnley)   m   Mary Queen of Scots
(1542–1567)

James VI of Scotland (1567–1625)
who also was James I (1603–1625) of England

Charles I (1625–1649)

Cromwell and the Commonwealth (1649–1660)

Charles II (1660–1685)

James II (1685–1688)

Mary II
(1688–1694)

Anne
(1702–1714)

The Tudor & Stuart family trees

showing the succession to the English throne

Study the family tree above, and then answer these questions.

1. Who was Elizabeth I's aunt?

2. What relation was Mary I to James V?

3. Who were the grandparents of Mary Queen of Scots?

4. For how many years was Henry VIII king?

5. Rank order these monarchs in order of the length of their reign, starting with the shortest: Henry VIII, Elizabeth I, Mary I, Mary Queen of Scots, James II.

ACTIVITY

Draw either your own family tree, or the family tree of somebody you know well. Include at least three generations.

EDWARD VI

Once Henry had made himself Head of the Church in England, the Pope was to be known as the Bishop of Rome. But Henry still did not agree with Martin Luther's teachings, so no change was made in the doctrines of the Church. In fact Henry's Parliament passed the **Statute of the Six Articles** which protected Catholic beliefs and worship. It was Edward VI, Henry's son and successor as King of England, who brought the Reformation to England. Edward was only 9 years old when he became king. He was a keen Protestant and during his reign made many changes to the Church, including:

1. The Statute of the Six Articles was cancelled.

2. A revised prayer book was issued in 1549 and written in English, not Latin.

3. Statues and paintings were taken out of the churches and shrines to Saints were destroyed.

4. Church services were held in English, not Latin.

The appearance of a church before (left) and after (right) the Reformation.

After these changes had been made, church buildings looked very different. The left picture shows a church as it would have looked before the Reformation, while the right picture shows how the same church would have looked like after the changes made by Edward VI.

What differences can you see between these two pictures? Why do you think the new church would have wanted to make these changes?

ACTIVITY

During the Reformation many paintings, statues and other pieces of art were destroyed by the Reformers. The reformers argued that these items were being worshipped like idols, and that destroying them could save people's souls. Do you think their reasons justified their actions? Discuss this question in your class.

MARY I

Edward died after only six years as King and his half sister Mary Tudor became Queen Mary I. Like her mother, Mary was Roman Catholic and she began restoring Catholicism to England:

1. Church services were again held in Latin, not English.

2. Statues, altars and stained glass windows were putback into churches.

3. 1554 the Pope became Head of the Church again.

Mary Tudor made herself very unpopular. Firstly, she married the Catholic Philip II of Spain and secondly by her policy of giving Protestants the choice of turning back to Catholicism or being burnt at the stake, sometimes called the 'turn or burn' policy. About 300 Protestants were burnt at the stake during Mary's five year reign gaining her the nickname ' Bloody Mary'.

ELIZABETH I

Mary died from illness in 1558 and her half sister Elizabeth became Queen: the last of Henry's children. Elizabeth was a Protestant but her religious feelings were not as strong as her brother or sister. She agreed to steer a middle road to satisfy both Catholics and Protestants. To please Protestants all churches had to use an English prayer book and clergymen were allowed to marry. To please Catholics, Priests were allowed to wear the traditional, elaborate robes and she was to be called **Governor** of the Church of England, rather than the **Head**. Her efforts did not impress the Pope who excommunicated Elizabeth in 1570. From that point on she is regarded as a Protestant.

The table shows the religious changes that took place in England between the time of Henry VIII and that of Elizabeth I.

	Henry VIII	Edward VI	Mary I	Elizabeth I
Religion	Catholic	Protestant	Roman Catholic	Protestant
Head of the Church	The King	The King	The Pope	The Monarch was only the 'Governor'
Language of services	Latin	English	Latin	English
Bible	English	English	English	English
Prayers	Mostly in Latin	English prayer book	Latin; new prayer book banned	English prayer book
Priests and marriage	Could not marry	Could marry	Forced to leave wives	Could marry

ACTIVITY

Draw a spider diagram showing each of Henry's children, their mother, the order they became monarch, and the religious changes they brought. Start like this:

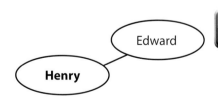

ACTIVITY

Draw a flow-chart of the religious changes that took place in England between 1527 and 1603.

RELIGIOUS PROBLEMS

Those who refused to accept this new Elizabethan church were called **recusants**. Many of them had to pay heavy fines for non-attendance at the Protestant church; others even lost their lands. Many Roman Catholic missionary priests came to England and were persecuted for trying to spread their message there. The Queen's Principal Secretary, Sir Francis Walsingham, led the campaign against these priests. Here are what two historians say about Walsingham:

> *Walsingham shows in his behaviour unmistakable marks of brutality and fanaticism. Blinded by religious passion he believed every Catholic priest was dangerous to the state and he conducted their examination in person.*
>
> England and the Catholic Church Under Persecution, AO Mayer, 1916

> *Walsingham was, on the whole, opposed to the execution of priests 'saving a few for example's sake'. Taken as a whole his policy was a policy of mercy. The result of his advice eased considerably the fate of the missionary priest.*
>
> Quoted in: Elizabeth in Danger, SM Harrison, Macmillan, 1990

RECUSANT: a person who refused to accept a new religion

WAINSCOT: wooden panelling around the walls of a room

Identify those words or phrases which show how these two writers differ about Walsingham's treatment of Catholic priests. Why might two historians disagree about a particular person or event?

The persecution did not discourage many and in the homes of wealthy recusants **priest hides** were built. You can see an example of one in the picture. This is what one priest said about having to spend time in a priest hide when people were looking for him:

> *Concealed in a cupboard behind the wainscot of a room for a few days ... at the end of that time ... [I] was released from the hiding hole half dead..*
>
> Father Gerard, a missionary priest describing his personal experience.

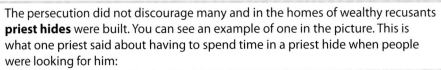

If a priest was caught, he could be imprisoned or tortured. This is how one priest described his experience in the Tower of London:

> *Of the means or instruments of torture employed in the Tower there are seven different kinds. The first is the Pit, a subterraneous cave twenty feet deep and entirely without light. The second is a cell or dungeon so small as to be incapable of admitting a person in erect posture ... The third is the rack, on which ... the limbs of the sufferer are drawn in opposite directions. The fourth is called the 'scavenger's daughter'. It consists of an iron ring which brings the head, feet and hands together until they form a circle. The fifth is the iron gauntlet, which encloses the hand with the most excruciating pain. The sixth consists of chains or manacles attached to the arms, and the seventh of fetters by which the feet are confined.*
>
> Edward Rishton, a priest imprisoned in the Tower of London

A priest's hide.

ACTIVITY

Rank order the seven different kinds of torture used in the Tower with number one being the worst.

Do you think this was a good way to convince people to become Protestant?

THE ELIZABETHAN THEATRE

A more pleasant side to life in Elizabethan England was the development of the theatre, most notably the plays of **William Shakespeare**. Many playhouses were built in London and around the country, the most famous of which was the *Globe Theatre* in London. A flag on top of the theatre indicated that a play would be performed that day. The early plays were performed in inn yards and this was reflected in the shape of these new theatres. Women were not permitted to act, so young boys always played the female parts.

The *Globe Theatre*, 1612

The early plays performed in inn yards often caused problems of crowd control. The audience was tightly packed and drink was widely available. On occasions, there was so much trouble at these plays that the London authorities banned them.

Some reasons for banning inn yard plays were:

• Disorderly conduct, especially by the young;
• Fights have broken out;
• Plays encourage immorality;
• Plays keep people from going to church;
• They are a waste of money;
• Pickpockets are encouraged to operate during plays;
• The collapse of temporary stages leads to injuries;
• Plague spreads among the closely packed audiences.

Because they were limited in scenery and lighting, words describing these were usually included in the plays, for example:

> *But look, the morn, in russet mantle clad, walks o'er the dew of yon high eastward hill.*
>
> *Hamlet*, William Shakespeare

Inside of the modern *Globe* replica

What time of day is being described in this quote from Hamlet?
What sort of terrain is being described?

ACTIVITY

You are a teenager who has just been to an evening play in an inn yard. Write a diary entry describing your experience.

The *Globe Theatre* was demolished in 1644, but in 1997 a replica was opened in London. It is open to the public and regularly puts on plays.

How do you think the designers of the new *Globe* were able to work out what the old one looked like (on both the inside and outside)? What sources would they have used? Are there any things they could not have found out?

EARLY VOYAGES

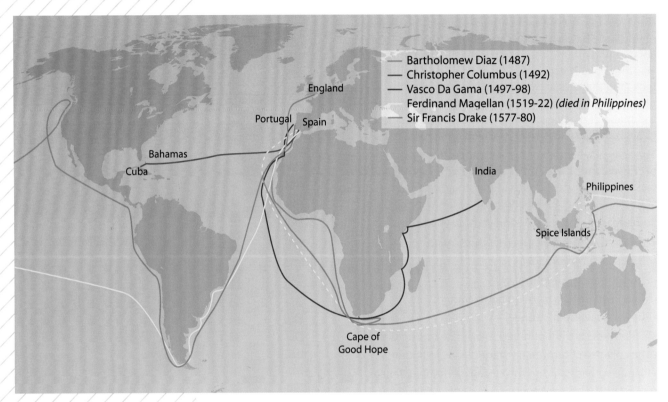

— Bartholomew Diaz (1487)
— Christopher Columbus (1492)
— Vasco Da Gama (1497-98)
— Ferdinand Magellan (1519-22) *(died in Philippines)*
— Sir Francis Drake (1577-80)

The voyages of five explorers. You will study Sir Francis Drake in Unit 10.

As European countries became more powerful, they looked for new territories and also new routes to bring goods from these places to Europe. This involved sailing further and further from Europe. To understand how this affected Europe we need to go back a bit, to the late fifteenth century.

In 1487 a Portuguese sailor called **Bartholomew Diaz** set sail from Lisbon and travelled south, going further than any other sailor had before. In early January 1488 a storm blew his ships off course and Diaz discovered that he had passed the southern tip of Africa, which he named 'Cape of Storms'. On his return to Portugal, the King renamed it 'Cape of Good Hope'.

Another Portuguese sailor, **Vasco Da Gama**, set sail from Lisbon in July 1497. It was his intention to sail past the Cape of Good Hope and reach India. Once he had succeeded in doing this, other sailors found their way to the Spice Islands (modern Indonesia). All of this helped Portugal to become a great empire. This is an entry from Da Gama's diary of 1498, listing some of the things he brought back to Portugal:

> *Da Gama got ready the following things to bring to the King of Calicut: twelve pieces of lambel, four scarlet hoods, six hats, four strings of coral, six wash-hand basins, a case of sugar, two casks of oil and two of honey.*

CHRISTOPHER COLUMBUS

Christopher Columbus was a poor Italian sailor. Many people at this time knew that the world was round, and Columbus wished to make a fortune by sailing westwards to find another route to the Spice Islands. The King of Portugal turned him down but he got support from the King and Queen of Spain.

Columbus had three ships for his voyage – the *Santa Maria*, the *Pinta* and the *Niña*. They left Spain in August 1492, sailing west across the Atlantic Ocean. In October they reached an island which Columbus named San Salvador (The Holy Saviour). He had actually reached the Bahamas, but Columbus thought he had arrived in India so he called the lands he had found the 'West Indies'. He sailed to Cuba where he saw men 'eating smoke'. On this first voyage he also visited the island of Hispaniola. This is what he said about the native people he saw:

> *The natives go as naked as when their mothers bore them. They are very well made ... their hair is short and coarse. I believe that they will easily become Christians because they seem to have no religion of their own ... I think they would make good servants because I noticed how quickly they understood what was said to them.*

What do you think the people "eating smoke" were really doing?

On his second voyage, in 1493, Columbus visited many islands including Antigua, Montserrat and St Kitts. He established a settlement in Hispaniola but treated the native population very badly, demanding valuable goods to be brought to him and delivering harsh punishments when he was not obeyed.

Columbus encouraging his men on their voyage to the New World.

On his third voyage, in 1498, he visited the island of Trinidad and the coast of South America at Venezuela. All this time he was convinced he was travelling along the coast of Asia. He returned to the colony he had left in Hispaniola and found the people there unhappy, as the conditions they were experiencing were not as Columbus had led them to believe. He allowed the native population to be enslaved and also hanged some of his crew for disobedience.

Columbus set off on his fourth voyage in 1502. He wanted to improve his reputation. He eventually arrived at Panama and survived a hurricane:

> *For nine days I was as one lost, without hope of life. Eyes never beheld the sea so angry, so high, so covered with foam. The wind not only prevented our progress, but offered no opportunity to run behind any headland for shelter; hence we were forced to keep out in this … ocean, seething like a pot on a hot fire. Never did the sky look more terrible; for one whole day and night it blazed like a furnace, and the lightning broke with such violence that each time I wondered if it had carried off my spars and sails; the flashes came with such fury and frightfulness that we all thought that the ship would be blasted. All this time the water never ceased to fall from the sky; I do not say it rained, for it was like another deluge. The men were so worn out that they longed for death to end their dreadful suffering.*

Account of Christopher Columbus quoted in "Admiral of the Ocean Sea: A Life of Christopher Columbus", SE Morison, 1942.

ACTIVITY

You are a newspaper reporter sent to cover the arrival of Columbus' ships in Panama. Make notes as you watch the ships arrive. Then interview (a) the cabin boy (b) the cook (c) the helmsman and (d) Christopher Columbus. From your notes write a report for your newspaper. Word process your report and remember to write a good headline. Draw at least one picture to illustrate your report.

Read the extract about Columbus surviving the hurricane and answer the questions:

1. What two difficulties did the strength of the wind cause?
2. Find two similies in this passage.
3. What factors would cause the "dreadful suffering" of the men?
4. For how long did the flashes of lightning occur?
5. What do you think Columbus means by "I do not say it rained, for it was like another deluge"?
6. Do you think this is a good description of a storm at sea? Why do you think so?

They were told of an area with lots of gold, but the weather was so extreme when they set sail that they eventually landed in Jamaica where they were stranded for a year, as the governors of nearby islands were not willing to help Columbus or his men. With some help from the native population Columbus returned to Spain in 1504. In his later years, Columbus demanded that the Spanish Crown give him 10% of all profits made in the new lands, but his demands were rejected. After his death, his heirs again sued the Crown for a part of the profits from trade with America, as well as other rewards.

On 20 May 1506, at about age 55, Columbus died. He was fairly wealthy from the gold his men had accumulated in Hispaniola. However, he never realised that he had discovered the 'New World' of the Americas, and he was disappointed not to have gained great wealth for the Spanish King and Queen by finding a route to Asia.

Columbus was the first person to bring cocoa beans to Europe. He didn't think they were very important: he thought they were a type of almond. But he wrote that the natives "seemed to hold these almonds at great price, for when they were brought on board ship together with their goods, I observed that when any of these almonds fell, they all stooped to pick it up, as if an eye had fallen".

What are cocoa beans used to make today?

ACTIVITY

Form a group of four. One pair should select a series of points supporting Columbus as a successful explorer; the second pair should draw up a list of points suggesting Columbus was a failure. The group should discuss these points and decide whether they believe Columbus was a success or failure.

Now present this information for access in your school library. Perhaps you can make a video presentation or PowerPoint display. You may prefer a written article to be filed or a series of posters to display.

FERDINAND MAGELLAN

Although these voyages helped persuade people that the world was round rather than flat, no one had actually *proved* that the world was round. The first sailor to circumnavigate the world was another Portuguese, Ferdinand Magellan. King Charles V of Spain agreed to support him. He set sail in April 1519. Magellan had five ships: the *Santiago*, *Victoria*, *Conception*, *Trinity* and *San Antonio*. Magellan sailed on the Trinity which weighed 110 tonnes. By contrast, the modern *Stena Caledonia*, which sails the Belfast–Stranraer route, weighs about 12,000 tonnes.

CIRCUMNAVIGATE: to go all the way round something

They took along enough food for two years. For example, the *Victoria* had:

2 tonnes dried biscuits	82 casks wine
1 tonne salted meat and fish	50 bundles garlic
½ tonne beans, lentils and peas	almonds & honey
216 kg cheese	4 crates marmalade
13.5 kg mustard	3 basket figs
8.5 kg sugar	8 barrels dried plums
30 barrels anchovies	

MUTINIES: rebellions against authority

After an eventful journey with mutinies and the loss of four ships, the *Victoria* sailed into Seville in Spain in September 1522 with only 18 men on board, all of them sick. The Italian crewman, Pigafetta, kept a journal and he described the death of Magellan in the Philippines in April 1521:

> *The Captain General was shot through the right arm with a poisoned arrow ... so many of [the natives] attacked the Captain General that they knocked his helmet off twice ... He always stood firm like a good knight ... They charged at him again with bamboo spears and cutlasses until they had killed our mirror, our light, our comfort and our true guide.*
>
> Pigafetta, a crewman on the *Victoria*

1. In what ways was meat and fish preserved on board ship?
2. Why was there so much mustard and garlic?
3. What evidence is there that Pigafetta had a good opinion of Magellan?

ACTIVITY

You are living in the Philippines in 1521. Compose an e-mail to a friend on another island describing the arrival of Magellan and his men. What do you think of them?

Magellan's voyage, 1519–22, was the first journey around the world. The first Englishman to do so was Sir Francis Drake 1577–1580. You will learn about him later.

ACTIVITY

Make a table of all four explorers. Your table should include:

- Their nationalities;
- The countries who sponsored them;
- When they made their voyages;
- The places and seas they visited;
- The flag of their sponsor country.

POWER

Let us consider what makes one country more powerful than another. Three factors are particularly important:

COMPENSATE: make up for

- **Geographical size.** For example, compare the Holy Roman Empire with Venice on the map in Unit 1 (page 5).
- **Population**. A larger population allowed a ruler to have a bigger army, which gave them more power.
- **Wealth**. Trade made several countries very rich. This could compensate for being small in size or population. For this reason England and Venice, although small, could afford to have powerful navies. Spain and Portugal developed overseas empires in America.

In eastern Europe the most powerful states were Sweden, Poland, Russia and the Ottoman Empire. But we are going to look at western Europe, in which the following three states were powerful in 1570:

	Spain	France	Holy Roman Empire
Ruler	Philip II (1556-1598)	Charles IX (1560-1574)	Maximilian II (1564-1576)
Religion	Catholic	Mainly Catholic but with some Protestants	Both Catholics and Protestants
Economy	Mainly agriculture. Very wealthy due to silver imported from south America	Agriculture, trade and industry	Agriculture, trade and industry
Armed Forces	Large navy and powerful army	Good army and navy	Each state had its own army
Politics	Rival of France. Also controlled what is now the Netherlands and Belgium, and southern Italy	Rival of Spain	Maximilian was an Emperor of a loose federation of independent states. The Empire had little real unity.

ACTIVITY

 COM

 MI

TPD

 WO

You have been given three things that make a country powerful. With a partner or in small groups, think of as many other factors as you can, which make a country powerful. Put them in order of importance and discuss your reasons.

Compare your group's answers with the rest of the class. Try to come to class agreement on their order of importance.

Then place Spain, France and the Holy Roman Empire in order of most to least powerful.

DYNASTIC WARS

Each European state was ruled by a royal family (or dynasty) which handed on the crown from father to son. The most powerful family in Europe was the Habsburg family whose emperor had been Charles V (1519–1556). Charles had ruled all the Habsburg territories but in later life he gave up the throne, and the family's land was split between his son Philip, who became King Philip II of Spain, and his brother Ferdinand, who became Holy Roman Emperor.

The main challenge to the power of the Habsburgs came from the Valois dynasty in France. There had been many wars involving other countries because of alliances and marriages. Henry VIII had married a Spanish princess (Catherine of Aragon) while Philip II of Spain had married Henry's daughter Mary, and tried to marry her sister, Elizabeth.

There were many civil wars in France, often caused by religion. On 24 August 1572, St Bartholomew's Day, there was a massacre of French Protestants in Paris and other places. Estimates of the numbers of deaths vary from 6,000 to 50,000 in just a few days.

CIVIL WAR: between two groups within a country

A contemporary drawing of the massacre of St Bartholomew's Day.

TPD

What does the picture tell us about the massacre?

How useful are pictures such as this to a historian?

Explain your answer.

MI

TPD

RESEARCH

The French Protestants were called 'Huguenots'. Many of them later came to Britain and Ireland. Research the Huguenots. Summarise the main points of their history, including why they left France. Some surnames in use here today came here because of the Huguenots. Try to find some examples.

RELIGIOUS WARS

The Reformation caused bitter divisions between Protestants and Catholics throughout Europe. In 1534 a priest called Ignatius Loyola formed the **Society of Jesus (Jesuits)** to re-convert people in Protestant countries. In other countries such as Spain and Italy, where there were few Protestants, a sort of religious court of law, called **The Inquisition**, was used to try to stamp out this 'new' religion of Protestantism. Terrible tortures were used, including the burning at the stake of people who would not conform.

UNIT 8: MARY QUEEN OF SCOTS

MARY'S EARLY LIFE

Mary Queen of Scots was born in Scotland in 1542, the daughter of the Scottish King James V and his Queen, a French princess, Mary of Guise. James was already near death, worn out by the intrigues of France, England and his own noblemen. He died when Mary was less than a week old. When he received the news of her birth he recalled how the throne had come to his family through Margery Bruce: "It came with a lass, and it will gang [go] with a lass." Then he laughed and fell back dead. Mary became Queen of Scotland when she was six days old, perhaps history's youngest Queen. She was to live for 45 turbulent years: a troubled life of disastrous marriages, intrigues, murders, plots and eventually imprisonment and execution.

Mary of Guise tried to rule Scotland as regent for her young daughter. Mary was betrothed to Francis, the four year old son of the French King Henry II, and her mother then sent Mary to live in France at the age of six (1548). They were married ten years later in 1558. A French writer called Brantôme wrote this about Mary about 1558:

> *She had a marvellous way of talking – gentle and feminine, and with kindly majesty. Her speech was modest and reserved, and very graceful. When she spoke Scottish (which is a very barbarous, ill-sounding and rough language) she made it sound beautiful and pleasant – which no one else can.*

Francis, aged about 14.
Painted by François Clouet.

Mary Queen of Scots, painted wearing mourning clothes after the death of her husband in 1560. Painted about 1560 by François Clouet.

REGENT: someone who rules a kingdom while the monarch is too young

BETROTHED: promise to marry at a later date

At this time, queens wore white, not black, when mourning.

MA

TPD

1. Assuming Francis is 14 years old in the picture, what year would it have been painted?

2. Why might Mary's mother have sent her to France after she was betrothed?

ACTIVITY

Write down as many words as you can to describe how the six-year-old Mary might have felt when she was sent away to France.

In 1559, Henry II was killed in a tournament accident and Francis became King, which made Mary the Queen of France. Her glory was shortlived, however, as her young husband fell sick and died in 1560. At the age of 18, Mary was a widow. Back in Scotland her mother also died in 1560. No longer Queen of France, Mary decided to return to Scotland in 1561.

MARY AS QUEEN OF SCOTLAND
The Scottish Reformation

In Scotland things had been changing. The old alliance with France was no longer popular. England had become Protestant and in Scotland many of the noblemen had converted to Protestantism, including Mary's half-brother James Stewart. (Mary used the French version of her name – Stuart.) They now wanted Scotland to be allied to England, rather than Catholic France. The Reformation in England had been briefly halted during the reign of Mary I (1553–58), who was Roman Catholic. (This was Mary Tudor, not to be confused with Mary Queen of Scots.)

But in 1558 the Protestant Elizabeth I (1558–1603) had become Queen of England. The Scottish nobles did not want a Catholic Queen, and Mary Queen of Scots was a practising Catholic. As soon as Mary arrived in Scotland there was opposition. The fiercest opposition came from **John Knox**, a fiery Protestant preacher, who was highly critical of Mary. He gave her strong advice on how she should dress and who she should marry. He did not like women to be in a position of authority, and wrote:

> *To promote a woman to bear rule, superiority, dominion or empire over any realm, nation or city is repugnant to nature and contumely (insulting) to God. It is a thing most contrary to his revealed will and approved ordinance (decree). Finally, it is the subversion of good order, equity and justice.*
>
> *The First Blast of the Trumpet Against the Monstrous Regiment of Women,*
> John Knox, 1558

How do the views of Knox differ from those of Brantôme regarding Mary? Explain why the two men might have viewed her differently.

The next eight years were the most important in Mary's life. Scandal seemed to pursue her wherever she went. Mary did not persecute the Protestants, but she remained Catholic herself. In 1565 she married **Henry, Lord Darnley**, a handsome 18 year old Roman Catholic, who was also her cousin. They had a son who became **James VI of Scotland** and later **James I of England**. The marriage strengthened Mary's claim to the English throne because she and her husband were both grandchildren of Henry VIII's sister Margaret Tudor (see the family tree in Unit 3). Darnley was proclaimed King of Scotland, ruling alongside Mary.

THE MURDER OF RIZZIO

Darnley turned out to be lazy, arrogant and spoilt. In 1566 he led a plot to murder David Rizzio, the Queen's Italian secretary and musician. Darnley was convinced that Rizzio was Mary's secret lover.

Armed men burst into the Queen's apartment and dragged Rizzio screaming into the hall where he was stabbed and hacked to death. The body suffered 56 stab wounds. Mary stayed with Darnley until their son James was born, but she had now fallen in love with the Earl of Bothwell, a dashing young soldier. On 9 February 1567 Darnley was lying ill at a house on the outskirts of Edinburgh called Kirk O'Fields. The house was blown up and the body of both Darnley and his servant were found strangled in the garden.

The murder of Rizzio, painted by Sir William Allan in 1833

Look at the painting of the murder of Rizzio.

1. What is the mood conveyed in this painting?
2. Is this a primary or a secondary source?

Imagine you want to paint a picture of the murder of Rizzio and you want your work to be as accurate as possible. How would you go about finding out the details of something that happened nearly 500 years ago?

A sketch showing Darnley's body at Kirk O'Fields in 1567, probably commissioned by an advisor to Elizabeth I to show her what happened.

Q The sketch of Kirk O'Fields is a sixteenth century drawing of a crime scene. What is the equivalent of this sketch today? Why do you think Elizabeth might have wanted a picture, and not just a written account of what happened?

Rumours swept Edinburgh that Bothwell and even the Queen were involved in the murder of Darnley. Despite this, Mary married Bothwell three months later. This led to an immediate rebellion. Mary was captured and imprisoned in Lochleven Castle, and her infant son James was proclaimed James VI. But Mary escaped in May 1568 and arrived in England to throw herself on the mercy of her cousin, Elizabeth I.

ACTIVITY

Create a timeline of the events of the life of Mary Queen of Scots up to 1568 for your classroom wall. Illustrate it with drawings.

THE PROBLEM OF MARY QUEEN OF SCOTS

The arrival of Mary Queen of Scots in England caused major problems for Queen Elizabeth I. Here are some of the reasons:

1. Elizabeth could hardly refuse political sanctuary for her own cousin.

2. Since Elizabeth was unmarried and had no children, Mary was her heir. Of course, Elizabeth was 35 and might yet marry.

3. The French had recognised Mary as Queen of England. Look at the family tree in Unit 3 again. Because Catholics did not believe Henry VIII was legitimately married to his second wife Anne Boleyn, they regarded Elizabeth as the daughter of his mistress and so not entitled to be Queen. Thus to Catholics, Mary Queen of Scots was the rightful heir of Mary I (Mary Tudor).

4. If Mary was allowed to live in England unrestricted, English Catholics might be tempted to rebel against Elizabeth and make Mary Queen.

5. Mary's son James was being brought up as a Protestant. If Elizabeth sent Mary back to Scotland it could result in a Catholic Queen north of the border, instead of a Protestant King. Alternatively, the Scots might kill Mary.

6. If she sent Mary to France, Catholic powers might invade England in an attempt to make Mary Queen.

7. The easy way out might be to execute Mary – but on what grounds? She had committed no crime in England. In any case, if a Queen executed another Queen it might set a precedent.

> SANCTUARY: a safe place to stay
>
> PRECEDENT: an example that others might copy

Elizabeth was careful never to meet Mary face to face. Instead she had the charges against Mary investigated, but the investigation neither proved Mary guilty of involvement in Darnley's murder, nor innocent either. Mary was allowed to stay in England as a 'guest' of Elizabeth, but in reality she was a prisoner, held in various castles against her will. During this time Mary was the focus of a number of plots against Elizabeth. This was a dangerous time for Elizabeth internationally. Catholic Spain was now an enemy of England, and Elizabeth was secretly aiding Protestants in the Netherlands who were rebelling against Spain. The Pope regarded Elizabeth as a heretic and in 1570 issued a **Papal Bull**. Part of this is quoted below:

Mary in captivity in England.

> *We declare the aforesaid Elizabeth to be excommunicated by the Church. Moreover, we declare that Elizabeth's title as Queen of England is false. No English nobles or subjects need keep their promises of loyalty or obedience to her. No one may obey her orders...*
>
> Extract from the Papal Bull of 1570

Q How can we tell that Elizabeth I's position with her Catholic subjects would be be threatened by the Papal Bull?

RESEARCH

What is a Papal Bull?

Answer this question, using the following headings:

Who issues it; How it gets its name; What it is written on; How it is sealed; Two examples of Papal Bulls; The words with which they start, in English and in Latin; The first line, in Latin, of an imaginary Papal Bull issued by a Pope called 'Paulus'.

ACTIVITY

In groups, construct a prosecution and a defence case for Mary Queen of Scots, who is accused of treason (ie, of killing the King of Scotland). One representative from each group is to put their case to the rest of the class.

ACTIVITY

EITHER Write a letter from Mary Queen of Scots to Elizabeth, protesting her innocence and asking for Elizabeth's sympathy and help.

OR Write a letter from Elizabeth to her most trusted adviser, explaining her dilemma about how to deal with Mary.

Queen Elizabeth I

ACTIVITY

Contemporary paintings can be valuable primary sources for an historian. In pairs, look at the clothes that Queen Elizabeth is wearing in this portrait. Remember there were no sewing machines at this time! Make a list of your observations in a table like this:

Observation	Possible conclusion
Her hair is very elaborately styled.	She could not have dressed it herself so she must have had help

When you have finished, write about 100 words describing what you can conclude about Elizabeth's way of life, just by looking at this painting.

ACTIVITY

Form into groups of about four. You have to write a short scene about an imaginary meeting between Mary Queen of Scots and Elizabeth I. Where might they meet? What might they say to each other? Would they be friendly or hostile? How would they part? Remember that they would probably have attendants with them who would also be included in your scene. When you have written your scenes, perhaps they could be performed in class. There could be a vote on which is the best!

MARY IS CHARGED

From this time on the number of plots involving Mary increased. Here are some of them:

1571 Ridolfi Plot. Ridolfi (an Italian) planned to marry Mary to the Duke of Norfolk, and replace Elizabeth with her. In 1572 Norfolk was beheaded.

1572 St Bartholomew's Day Massacre in France. This was begun by the Guises, Mary's French relatives (see Unit 7).

1584 Assassination of William the Silent, the Protestant ruler of the Netherlands. This frightened the English government, who called for Mary to be executed.

In 1572 Parliament thought they had enough evidence to bring charges against Mary:

1. *That she has wickedly and untruly challenged the present estate and possession of the crown of England and ... usurped the style and arms of the same.*

2. *That she has ... sought by subtle means to withdraw the late Duke of Norfolk from his natural obedience and against Her Majesty's express prohibition to couple herself in marriage with the said Duke, to the intent that thereby she might ... bring to effect Her Majesty's ... destruction.*

3. *That she has ... stirred ... the Earls of Northumberland and Westmorland ... to rebel and levy open war against Her Majesty.*

4. *That she has practised ... to procure new rebellion to be raised within this realm. And for that intent she made choice of one Ridolphi, a merchant of Italy, who ... solicited the said wicked enterprises to the Pope and other ... confederates beyond the Seas.*

Charges made by Parliament against Mary Queen of Scots in May 1572

Why did Elizabeth's attitude to Mary change after 1572?

Elizabeth could not bring herself to harm Mary, so **Sir Francis Walsingham** (Elizabeth's secretary) set up a trap for her. A young Catholic, **Anthony Babington**, was persuaded to pass secret messages from Mary to a continental 'agent' (who was in fact a spy for Walsingham). The picture shows an example of the code for the messages. When the trap was sprung there was enough proof to find both Babington and Mary Queen of Scots guilty of treason.

One of the codes used in the Babington Plot.

ACTIVITY

Use the Babington code to compose a short letter from Babington's continental 'agent', trying to encourage Mary to take part in a plot against Elizabeth.

Mary was tried in October 1586 at Fotheringay Castle, but it was February 1587 before Elizabeth was persuaded to sign the death warrant. The execution took place on 8 February at Fotheringay. This is an account of her execution:

> With a smiling face she turned to her men servants standing upon a bench (behind the platform). They were weeping. The Queen bid them farewell.
> She kneeled down upon a cushion and prayed. Then, groping for the block with both her hands, she held them there. They would have been cut off had they not been espied (seen). Then she laid herself upon the block, most quietly. It took two strokes of the axe before he (the executioner) cut off her head. Then one espied a little dog which was under the (dead queen's) clothes. It could not be gotten out by force and afterwards would not depart the dead corpse but came and laid by the shoulders.
>
> A eyewitness account of the execution of Mary Queen of Scots, written by Robert Wyngfield.

This photograph shows all that remains of Fotheringay Castle in Northamptonshire. The grandson of Mary Queen of Scots, Charles I, became King of England in 1625, and Fotheringay was demolished in 1627.

Might the king have ordered the demolition himself? What motive might he have had?

Study the picture and the written account (opposite) of the execution of Mary Queen of Scots and answer the questions that follow.

1. What one important fact should an historian find out when seeing these sources for the first time?

2. Are there similarities between the picture and the written account?

3. What does the picture tell you that the written account does not?

4. What does the written account tell you that the picture does not?

5. What reason could there be for the presence of so many people in the room?

6. There is a bonfire in the picture. What do you think might be being burned and why?

At this time, a picture might show two events that happened one after the other, so the bonfire probably happened after the execution.

ACTIVITY

Class debate. Organise a class debate on the motion: "This house believes that Queen Elizabeth should not have executed Mary, Queen of Scots." Remember that, if you are arguing in favour of the motion, you must suggest actions that Elizabeth might have taken instead.

MARITIME RIVALRIES

By 1588 England had become one of the greatest naval powers in the world. This alone was enough to make England and Spain bitter rivals in the second half of the sixteenth century. The early voyages of discovery to Africa, Asia and the New World (America) had been by Portuguese and Spanish seamen. Columbus, who reached America in 1492, was financed by Spain, though he was Italian himself. In 1494 Spain and Portugal had signed a treaty dividing the New World between them. The New World had abundant resources of silver and gold and soon made Spain rich.

ACTIVITY

Most people in South America today speak either Spanish or Portuguese. On a blank map of South America, colour in the countries that speak Spanish in one colour, and the countries that speak Portuguese in different colour. What can this tell us about the history of these countries? In what other ways can you learn about a country's history by looking at it today?

After 1550 England began to get involved. English seamen began to trade with both west Africa and south America. At first this was peaceful. However Spanish law did not allow south America to trade with anyone other than Spain, and in 1567 a Spanish fleet attacked English ships, commanded by **Sir John Hawkins**, in San Juan de Ulua harbour in Mexico. From that time on English seamen regarded Spain as an enemy.

A modern replica of Drake's ship, *Golden Hind*

In Europe the two governments officially remained at peace, but piracy became common on the high seas. The most famous pirate was **Sir Francis Drake** who, in his ship the *Golden Hind*, sailed round the world in 1577–80. On this voyage he captured the treasure ship *Cacafuego* loaded with 26 tons of silver, 13 chests of gold coins and expensive cloth. When Drake got home, the Queen received a share of the loot and Drake was knighted. When the Spanish Ambassador protested to Elizabeth, she denied any knowledge of the event, but it was said at the time that as she was talking to him, the royal dressmaker was measuring her for a new dress in Spanish cloth of gold, stolen on the voyage!

KNIGHTED: Given the title 'Sir' or 'Dame' by the monarch

Queen Elizabeth knighting Sir Francis Drake (after the original by the Victorian artist Gilbert)

THE NETHERLANDS

Philip II, King of Spain had inherited the Netherlands from his father Emperor Charles V in 1555. The Netherlands, sometimes called the Seventeen Provinces, was wealthy because of the wool trade and cloth making. Flemish merchants had become rich through this trade. Philip II lived in the Netherlands until 1559, when he moved to Spain. Around the same time militant Protestantism was spreading in the Netherlands. A revolt against the rule of Philip II began in 1567. There were four main reasons for this:

FLEMISH: A name used at the time for people from the Netherlands. Also a language spoken today in Belgium

MILITANT: Active and aggressive in support of a cause

1. Philip II wanted to remove many of the privileges of the Seventeen Provinces, and govern them directly from the capital, Brussels.

2. Philip wanted to stamp out Protestantism in the Netherlands, and introduced the Jesuits and the Inquisition. He began burning Protestants at the stake. This also antagonised Flemish Catholics who were tolerant and did not want such extreme forms of persecution. In 1566 Protestants rioted, wrecking Catholic churches.

3. In 1567 Philip sent a large army to the Netherlands in a show of force, designed to put down opposition. This army began a reign of terror in Flanders.

4. The Spanish government imposed heavy taxes on the Netherlands to pay for this army.

ACTIVITY

Imagine you are a Protestant living in the Netherlands at this time. Write a letter to a friend in England explaining why you are angry with Philip II.

At first England gave only indirect help to the Netherlands. Elizabeth was anxious to avoid a full scale war with Spain. She saw France as a bigger danger to England. However, a Spanish victory in the Netherlands would have threatened England's own cloth trade, as well as removing a potential Protestant ally. In 1584 the leader of the revolt, William the Silent, was assassinated, and in 1585 Antwerp, an important port, fell to the Spanish. Elizabeth sent English troops to help the Dutch. Their arrival, in 1586, helped Philip II make up his mind to invade England.

ACTIVITY

In pairs or groups, list as many reasons as you can why Philip II of Spain may have been annoyed with Elizabeth I and England at this time. When you have a list, share it with the rest of the class. Then, as a class, decide which was the most important, and why you think this.

ACTIVITY

Look at a map of Europe today. Find: the Netherlands, Belgium, England and Spain. Do you think England or Spain is in a better location to fight a war in the Netherlands? Explain your answer.

Why do you think Elizabeth was anxious to avoid a war with Spain?

ACTIVITY

Make a Wall of War!

Have several pads of post-it notes available. Anyone can write on a note and stick it on the wall. You must think of things which are used in war. For example, cannon or submarines. When you have thought of all you can, arrange them into two categories: (a) war in the sixteenth century and (b) war today.

Discuss in class in which century you think war was most dangerous. Have any methods remained the same? What do you think is the biggest difference between fighting in the sixteenth century and the twenty-first century?

In the previous unit you learned about one of Elizabeth I's most successful pirates, Sir Francis Drake, who attacked ships and towns belonging to England's enemy Spain, and brought treasure back to his Queen. In this unit you will make an assessment of Sir Francis Drake.

ACTIVITY

In this unit are six sources giving contemporary accounts of the activities of Drake. Select points from these sources which support Drake as a brave adventurer and explorer, working for his Queen. Select other points which show him as a thief, seeking to obtain riches for himself.

When we came [to Valaparizo, in Chile], we found a ship at anchor, and on board eight Spaniards and three blacks, who thinking we were Spaniards and their friends, welcomed us with a drum and a bottle of Chilean wine to drink to us. But as soon as we entered, one of our company, called Thomas Moone... punched one of the Spaniards, and told him to get down. ... We made them all go below deck, all except one Spaniard, who suddenly leapt overboard into the sea, and swam ashore to the town of S.Iago, to warn them of our arrival. There were only nine houses in the town and they all fled, abandoning the town. Our General [Sir Francis Drake] took a small boat, along with a boat from the Spanish ship, and went to the town. When we came to it, we searched it, and found a small chapel, which we entered and found a silver chalice, two ornamental bottles and an altar cloth, which our General gave to Mr Fletcher, his Minister.

Account of a raid on a Spanish town in Chile, 1580, from *Purchas his Pilgrimes*, Samuel Purchas, 1625

Once we were at sea, our General [Drake] searched the [Spanish] ship, and found a large amount of Chilean wine, and 25,000 Pezos of very pure and fine gold, amounting in value to more than 37,000 Dukats of Spanish money. We then went to the port of Tarapaca, and once we had landed we found a Spaniard sleeping by the sea, and beside him thirteen bars of silver, which weighed 4,000 Spanish Duckats. We took the silver, and left the man. Not far from there, going on land to look for fresh water, we met a Spaniard and an Indian boy driving eight llamas [which each] had on its back two leather bags, each of which contained 50 pounds of fine silver. Upon bringing both the llamas and their cargo to the ships, we found a total of 800 pounds of silver. Then we sailed to a place called Arica, and once we entered the port, we found three small boats, which we searched, and in one of them found 57 wedges of silver, each of them weighing about 20 pounds. Every of the these wedges was the size of a brick. We found no-one on any of these boats… But our General, content with what we had taken from the ships, left the town, and went back to sea, and set sail for Lima [in Peru].

Account of some other raids carried out by Drake, from *Purchas his Pilgrimes*, Samuel Purchas, 1625

We arrived at Lima [and] found about twelve ships anchored there. Our General searched these ships, and found in one them a chest full of silver coins, and large amounts of silk and linen. On this ship he heard about another ship, called the Cacafuego, which had sailed towards Paita, and that which was laden with treasure. On discovering this, we stayed there no longer but, after cutting all the anchor chains of the ships in the harbour… and at full speed we followed the Cacafuego… On the way we met a small boat laden with ropes and rigging for ships, which [our General] boarded and searched, and found in her 80 pounds of gold, a gold crucifix with large emeralds set in it, which he took, along with some of the rope for his own ship. Then we continued on our way, still following the Cacafuego, and our General promised his crew that the man who first saw her would be given his gold chain. In the end it was John Drake, going up the mast, who spotted her at about three o'clock, and we reached her about six o'clock. We boarded the ship, after firing three cannonballs at her, which knocked down her mast. On board we found treasure consisting of jewels and precious stones, thirteen chests full of silver coins, 80 pounds of gold, and 26 tonnes of silver. All of this happened at a place called Cape de San Francisco, about 800 km from Panama.

Account of Drake's raid on the Cacafuego, from *Purchas his Pilgrimes*, Samuel Purchas, 1625

On the 21st of August we entered the Strait, which we found to have many dead ends and it looked as if there were no way through at all. We often had the wind against us, so that sometimes some of the fleet got past a cape or headland, but others were forced to turn back again, and to come to an anchor where they could. In this Strait there are many safe bays with lots of fresh water, but yet the water in the bays is so deep, that we were unable to reach the bottom with our anchor unless we stopped in a narrow river mouth. When extreme winds do come (and they are very common here) they carry with them great *danger. ... On the 24th of August we arrived at an island in the Straits, where we found huge numbers of flightless birds, the size of geese. We killed 3000 of them in less than a day, and thoroughly replenished our food stocks.*

Account of Drake's passage through the Strait of Magellan, from *Purchas his Pilgrimes,* Samuel Purchas, 1625

The most southern point in all these islands stands at 56° south, beyond which there is nothing to the south except the meeting place of the Atlantic Ocean and the South Sea. It has long been thought that these islands were an unknown land inhabited by many strange monsters. Indeed, it truly is an unknown land because before now maps and the descriptions of geographers do not say anything about it, either because they were deceived or because they were making things up. In fact, as far as we know, nobody knew anything about this land before our voyage.

Turning past [the southernmost cape] we sailed quickly, assuming the coast of Chile lay to our north west as shown on our maps. However, we found that it actually lay to the north east and east so it seems that this part of Chile has not previously been discovered, or at least not accurately mapped, for a distance of at least 12 degrees, either deliberately or because of ignorant conjecture.

Account of Drake's exploration of the coast of what is now North America, from *Purchas his Pilgrimes*, Samuel Purchas, 1625

We anchored in a bay and the local people, since they had their houses close to the sea, came to meet us and gave our General gifts. They were amazed at the things we showed to them but our General (such is his natural humanity) treated them courteously and gave them clothes with which to cover their nakedness. At this point they decided we were gods, and we could not persuade them otherwise. The gifts which they gave to our General were feathers and nets. Their houses are made from circular mounds of earth, on top of which are long pieces of wood that meet at the top like a steeple and, because they are so close together, are very warm. Their beds are on the ground and lined with rushes, scattered around the houses which have a fire in the centre. The men do not wear any clothes, while the women wear skirts made of something like hempe which hang loose from their hips. The women also wear deerskins on their shoulders, with their hair draped over it. The women are very obedient and helpful to their husbands.

Account of Drake's exploration of the coast of what is now North America, from *Purchas his Pilgrimes*, Samuel Purchas, 1625

ACTIVITY

Using the information in the account of Drake's exploration of the coast of North America, draw a picture illustrating how these people lived.

RESEARCH

In pairs or groups, your task is to meet as a Committee in the House of Commons, carry out research and produce a report for Queen Elizabeth I and her Council suggesting whether or not England should continue to support this sailor.

You should refer to the evidence in the Unit but also use evidence you have found elsewhere. Remember to note your sources and quote them at the end of your report to enable government advisors to check the accuracy of your advice. This is referred to as a **Bibliography**.

After you have discussed the problems and collated (put together) your evidence you can present your independent report as a file, PowerPoint presentation, or in another suitable format of your choice.

RELIGIOUS CONCERNS

In Unit 10 we saw how disagreements over piracy and the Netherlands harmed the relations between Spain and England. But there were also religious reasons, and Philip II had been keeping an eye on England for a long time. Spain and England had been allies in the time of Henry VII (1485–1509) and Henry VIII (1509–1547), but this had weakened with the Protestant Reformation in England during the reign of Edward VI (1547–53). However when Mary I, a Catholic, became Queen (1553–58) England returned to the Spanish camp. Philip II married Mary and, if the marriage had not been childless, England could have become part of the Spanish Empire. Mary's death in 1558 ended any such hopes since her younger sister Elizabeth I (1558–1603) was a Protestant. Philip asked Elizabeth to marry him, but she refused.

Philip II and Mary I. Painted by Hans Eworth in 1558.

Philip was convinced that the people of England were Catholic at heart, and he planned to overthrow Elizabeth and replace her with a Catholic monarch: perhaps Mary Queen of Scots, who was still alive at this time. The Spanish ambassador to England kept a close eye on the persecution of English Catholics and reported back to Philip regularly:

> *They [Parliament] have agreed already to a great persecution of the Catholics, who will not attend their churches, and have appointed a commissioner to proceed against them in person and estate.*
>
> Spanish Ambassador to Philip II, 12 August 1581

> *From what I understand, God has been pleased still to maintain some Catholics in this country, and I am told that many persons openly observe the religion, not withstanding the penalties against it.*
>
> Spanish Ambassador to Philip II, 31 March 1578

> *In accordance with the laws which I said had been passed in this parliament, they have begun to persecute the Catholics worse than ever before, both by condemning them to the £20 fine if they do not attend church every month and by imprisoning them closely in the gaols. The clergymen they succeed in capturing are treated with a variety of terrible tortures: amongst others is one torment that people in Spain imagine to be that which will be worked by Anti-Christ as the most dreadfully cruel of them all. This is to drive iron spikes between the nails and the quick; and two clergymen in the tower have been tortured in this way, one of them being Campion of the Company of Jesus, who, with the other was recently captured. I am assured that when they would not confess under this torture the nails of their fingers and toes were turned back; all of which they suffered with great patience and humility.*
>
> Spanish Ambassador to Philip II, 12 August 1581

What are the strengths and weaknesses of using only the Spanish ambassador's accounts of the treatment of English Catholics to assess this period?

A contemporary picture of torture in the sixteenth century.

ACTIVITY

This picture shows sixteenth century torture. How does the evidence in the letters from the Spanish ambassador and from this picture illustrate the cruelty which appears to be common in sixteenth-century Europe?

PHILIP AND THE POPE

For some time Philip had been asking the Pope for some time to give his blessing to a Spanish invasion of England. Philip claimed that if Spanish troops landed, thousands of Englishmen would flock to their support. This is a letter Philip wrote to his ambassador in Rome in 1587:

> *You will cautiously approach his Holiness [the Pope] and in such terms as you think fit endeavour to obtain from him a secret brief declaring that, failing the Queen of Scotland, the right to the English Crown falls to me ... You will impress upon his Holiness that I cannot undertake a war in England for the purpose merely of placing upon that throne a young heretic like the King of Scotland (James VI) who, indeed, is by his heresy incapacitated to succeed. His Holiness must, however, be assured that I have no intention of adding England to my own dominions, but to settle the crown upon my daughter, the Infanta.*
>
> Philip II to his Ambassador in Rome, 11 February 1587

1. Mary Queen of Scots had been executed on 8 February 1587, three days before this letter was written. Do you think this news had reached Philip? How can you tell?

2. Why did Philip II need the approval of the Pope to invade England?

The Pope was not sure about Philip II's motives. He was reluctant to offend Philip who was one of the foremost champions of the Catholic faith in Europe, but he suspected that Philip might have other motives, as well as a religious crusade, to overthrow Protestantism in England. The Pope did not want the power of Spain to get any greater.

Despite his doubts the Pope eventually felt he had no choice but to approve and bless Philip's invasion plan.

1. How can you tell from his letter to his ambassador in Rome that Philip II is anxious to make the Pope less suspicious of his motives?

2. Why do you think the Pope gave his approval to Philip's plan to attack England?

UNIT 13: THE ARMADA'S VOYAGE

PREPARATIONS

At first Philip planned to send a huge army to England directly from Spain, but he would have needed 500 ships and to do this would have been much too expensive. So Philip came up with a cheaper plan. This plan was to use the Spanish army already fighting in the Netherlands to invade England. These could be towed across the English channel in flat barges. They would be protected by a fleet of warships (called the **Armada**) and supply ships that would sail from Spain to accompany them.

These plans were frustrated by bad luck and by English military action:

1. In April 1587 Sir Francis Drake raided the Spanish port of Cadiz and destroyed 24 big Spanish ships, as well as supply ships.

2. Several supply ships carrying barrel staves were captured. Later the Armada was to suffer because food was stored in barrels made of unseasoned wood which made it go rotten.

3. Early in 1588 the commander of the Armada, Santa Cruz, died. His replacement, chosen for rank rather than experience, was the Duke of Medina Sidonia who had little knowledge of the sea.

4. The Spanish failed to capture a port in the Netherlands with deep enough water for the Armada ships.

> **BARREL STAVES: strips of wood used to make barrels**
>
>

ACTIVITY

TPD

WO

In pairs or groups, imagine you are advisors to Philip II. List the advantages and disadvantages of sending an Armada to attack Britain in 1588. Decide what advice you would give Philip II. Remember that you are Spanish – what opinion do you have of England? Would your personal feelings affect your advice?

THE ARMADA SAILS

An artist's impression of some of the Armada ships getting ready to sail.

On 20 May 1588 the Armada set sail from Lisbon in Portugal. It consisted of 130 ships, drawn from all parts of the Spanish Empire, including rowing galleys from the eastern Mediterranean, made up of 75 fighting ships, 25 large merchant ships, and 30 small sloops. They carried 10,000 sailors,

> **SLOOP: a small warship**
>
>

20,000 soldiers and over 2000 artillery pieces. In contrast the English were able to muster 102 warships, although only 25 of these were the best, 'first line' ships. You can see the progress of the Armada in this timeline.

20 May	9 June	19 July	19–27 July	27 July	28 July	29 July–3 Aug	Aug–Oct
May Set sail from Lisbon.	June Fleet dispersed by storm off Corunna. Month's delay to regroup.	English sighted the Armada off Cornwall. Beacon fires relayed the news to Plymouth and London.	Nine days battle up the English Channel. The Armada adopted a crescent formation with the English attacking from behind.	Spanish fleet anchored off Calais hoping for a week to take on fresh supplies.	Armada attacked in darkness by eight fireships (each English commander had given up his oldest ship and set fire to it). In panic many of the Spanish cut their anchors and headed out to sea.	Six day battle off the Kent coast. Several Spanish ships were sunk. The Spanish could not reach the Netherlands, land in England or regroup. They headed into the North Sea. Both sides ran low in ammunition and near the Scottish coast the English turned back.	Spanish fleet passed round Scotland and Ireland but was badly damaged by storm and high seas. At least 19 ships were wrecked off the Irish coast. Others were driven out into the Atlantic and foundered.

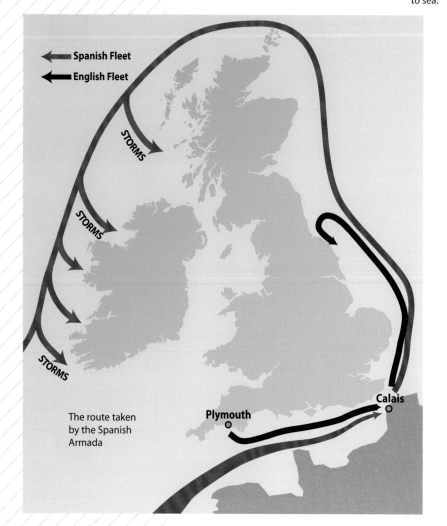

Spanish Fleet
English Fleet

STORMS

STORMS

STORMS

The route taken by the Spanish Armada

Plymouth

Calais

FOUNDER: sink by taking on water

COM

BC

ACTIVITY

It is 28th July 1588. You are a cabin boy on one of the Spanish ships which has anchored off Calais to take on supplies. Write an eyewitness account of what happened that evening and night. Use your imagination! Perhaps some accounts could be read out in class.

ACTIVITY

Try this. Draw or paint a picture of the battle between the Armada and the English fleet.

ACTIVITY

Using the timeline of the Armada, construct an **illustrated** timeline on your classroom wall.

The English felt so strongly about defeating the Armada that during the battle off the coast of Kent the English commanders signed a resolution declaring what they would do:

> *We whose names are hereunder written, have determined and agreed in council to follow and pursue the Spanish fleet until we have cleared our own coast and brought the firth west of us, and then to return back again, as well to restock our ships (which stand in extreme supplies) as also to guard and defend our own coast at home; with further protestation that, if our lack of food and munitions were supplied, we would pursue them to the furthest they have gone.*
>
> The Resolution of the Council of War of the English Commanders to fight against the Armada, 1 August 1588

In total, about a third of the Spanish ships were sunk. Another third were so badly damaged that they could never sail again. Medina Sidonia finally got back to Spain on 23 October, delirious from lack of water. A third of the men did not return.

ACTIVITY

As a class, list as many reasons as you can why the Spanish Armada failed in its mission of invading England. Once you have finished your list, rank them in order of importance starting with the most important. Which reason would have been regarded as most important by (a) Philip II (b) Elizabeth I.

A sixteenth century map of Ireland similar to the maps used by the Spanish.

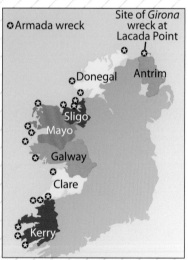

Ireland as it is in reality, with the seven counties with Armada wrecks marked.

In what ways was the information in the sixteenth century map unreliable? How important are sources like this in helping us to understand why so many ships were lost off the coast of Ireland?

SHIPWRECKS

Why were so many Spanish ships wrecked off the west coast of Ireland? Let us go back to what happened at Calais. When the fireships were sent towards the Armada on 28 July 1588, the Spanish ships had cut their anchors in panic. Most ships had at least one spare anchor, but if a ship is being carried towards land by a storm, such as the Armada faced off Ireland in September, it will drop anchor to avoid shipwreck. But the ships no longer had enough anchors.

Also, the Spanish thought Ireland looked like the map shown in the picture. They assumed that if you sailed round the top of Ireland heading west, you could turn south about ten miles past Donegal. But in reality, if you did that, you would find Sligo and Mayo in the way! With the wind blowing from the south west they could not get back out to sea again. Ten of the nineteen wrecks were off Mayo, Sligo and Donegal. Those Spaniards who did make it ashore found themselves robbed, stripped, beaten and sometimes killed by the local Irish people.

This table shows the 19 ships that sank off the coast of Ireland in 1588.

Ship	Ton	Soldiers	Sailors	Rowers	Guns	Wrecksite	Date
San Marcos	790	292	117	0	33	Clare	20 Sep
La Lavia	728	203	71	0	25	Sligo	25 Sep
La Rata Encoronada	820	335	84	0	35	Mayo	21 Sep
La Trinidad Valencera	1100	281	79	0	42	Donegal	16 Sep
La Anunciada	703	196	79	0	24	Clare	20 Sep
San Nicolas Prodaneli	834	274	81	0	26	Mayo	16 Sep
Juliana	860	325	70	0	32	Donegal	?
Santa Maria De Vision	666	236	71	0	18	Sligo	25 Sep
San Juan	530	163	113	0	24	Sligo	25 Sep
La Trinidad	872	180	122	0	24	Kerry	15 Sep
San Juan Bautista	652	192	93	0	24	Kerry	24 Sep
Girona	700	169	120	300	50	Antrim	28 Oct
El Gran Grin	1160	256	73	0	28	Clare	22 Sep
Urca Duquesa Santa Ana	900	280	77	0	23	Donegal	26 Sep
Santa Maria De La Rosa	945	225	64	0	0	Kerry	21 Sep
San Esteban	936	196	68	0	26	Clare	20 Sep
Falcon Blanco Mediano	300	76	27	0	16	Galway	25 Sep
Ciervo Volante	400	200	22	0	18	Mayo	22 Sep
Santiago	600	56	30	0	19	Mayo	21 Sep

1. A galley was a ship with oars and rowers. Which of the 19 ships was a galley?
2. List the five largest Armada wrecks in order, starting with the biggest.

ACTIVITY

Draw a bar chart showing how many ships sank in each county. Write the names of the seven counties along the x-axis. The y-axis will show the number of ships that sank in each one. Can you draw any conclusions from this?

Francisco de Cuellar was a high-ranking Spanish officer who survived the wreck of the *San Juan* in Sligo. He later wrote about his experience in Ireland:

> *I passed many Spaniards completely naked without any clothes at all, shivering with the cold that was very severe. The night came upon me in this dreary place and I lay down on some rushes ... a gentleman came up to me, naked, a very gentle youth. He was so frightened that he could not speak, not even to tell me who he was.*
> *...*
>
> *At daybreak I began to go towards a monastery ... but found it torn down, the church and holy images burnt and twelve Spaniards hanged within the Church by English Protestants who went about looking for us in order to kill all those who had escaped the hazard of the sea. I found nobody there except the Spaniards dangling from the iron grills in the church windows ... I went out very quickly.*

What words does Francisco de Cuellar use to describe what Ireland is like?

ACTIVITY

Class discussion

"Francisco de Cuellar was Spanish: therefore, what he wrote about Ireland must be unreliable." Discuss this statement in class. Do you agree or disagree? Why? Can you pick out anything in his account that seems odd?

The Girona

The most famous Armada wreck was that of the *Girona*. The *Girona* had managed to find refuge at Killybegs in Donegal, and had been joined there by the crew of two wrecked ships – *Santa Maria Encoronada* and *Duquessa Santa Ana*. The *Girona's* captain decided to over-winter in Scotland and turned back. He was heading east along the North Antrim coast when his ship was wrecked on 28 October at Lacada Point near the Giant's Causeway. Of the 1,300 on board, five survived.

In 1967 the wreckage of the *Girona* was located and divers salvaged hundreds of artifacts including cannon, an anchor, gold chains and jewellery. The ship itself had completely disappeared. The *Girona* treasure is now in the Ulster Museum in Belfast.

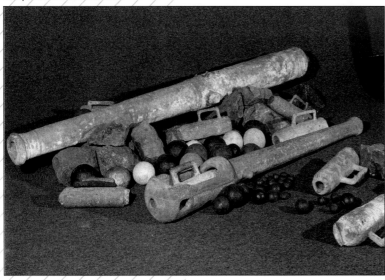
Weapons from the *Girona*.

The large cannon is a bronze 'half-baker'; the smaller one is a bronze 'esmeril' (swivel gun) containing a moving part called a breech block. Around them are more bronze breech blocks and different sizes of stone and iron shot.

Of what use is it to an historian to be able to see items from the *Girona* today?

ACTIVITY

Imagine you are a Spanish sailor who had survived the wreck of the *Duquessa Santa Ana* and are now on the *Girona*. Describe what happened up to this point, and then describe what happens next. Write about how you are feeling.

THE END OF THE WAR

The war between England and Spain continued after 1588, but the Armada was its climax. In 1598 Philip II died and in 1603 Elizabeth I died. Her successor, James I made peace with Spain in 1604.

RESEARCH

In groups, produce an illustrated report on the *Girona*. Sections of your report would be (a) what the *Girona* was (b) why it was wrecked (c) the discovery of the wreck (d) the salvage (e) assessment of the importance of the discovery (f) conclusion.

Word process your report neatly. Remember to include a title page and details of your sources at the end. Present your report in a simple binding.

Review this section

Take a look back over this section to remind yourself of all that you have learnt about.

Did anything specially interest you? If so, explain briefly to the class what you found interesting.

Did you find anything really boring?

ACTIVITY

Make a timeline

Starting at Unit 2 and finishing at Unit 14, create a timeline of all that happened during these years.

If you had to pick a time to live during these years, which year would you choose to be born in?

Take out the piece of paper where you noted your ideas on pirates at the beginning of this section. How accurate were your ideas?

Word Check

Check out these words to make sure you can spell them.

Fotheringay	Reformation	contemporary
execution	dynasty	rebellion
assassination	Huguenot	Antwerp
dilemma	Inquisition	ambassador
Babington	Columbus	
innocent	prosecution	

If you're not sure if you can spell any of them, check them out a few more times.

Class Quiz!

Divide into two teams and decide on a prize for the winning team. If you get a question right, your team gets a point, BUT if you get a question wrong, you lose a point! So think carefully before you answer.

1. Which of Henry VIII's six wives survived him?

2. Who was the king or queen before Elizabeth I?

3. How do you write the number 9 in Roman numerals?

4. Who wrote "The First Blast of the Trumpet Against the Monstrous Regiment of Women" in 1558?

5. What nationality was Christopher Columbus?

6. Who was Mary Queen of Scots second husband?

7. In what direction was the Girona sailing when it was shipwrecked?

8. Who made the first journey round the world?

9. What happened at Fotheringay Castle in 1587?

10. Where was the Globe Theatre?

11. Who was suspected of murdering Lord Darnley?

12. What was the name of Sir Francis Drake's ship?

13. What is the Latin phrase that means "Defender of the Faith"?

14. Who was the King of Spain at the time of the Armada?

15. Name three food items taken by Magellan on his voyage round the world.

16. "Elizabeth I wanted to return England to Catholicism". True or false?

17. What is a 'civil war'?

18. From what does the word 'Protestant' come from?

19. Why were priest hides needed?

20. What was Henry VIII's family surname?

Before you start, read this statement.

"Colonisation is the act, by a militarily strong country, of invading and taking over the sovereignty of another country or area, which then becomes known as a colony... Colonisation denies the sovereignty of the colonised country and the rule of law becomes that of the coloniser."

From: www.citystrolls.com/z-f-page/colonisation.htm, accessed 26 July 2011

Discuss this statement in class and work out exactly what it means. Do you agree with it?

. . . .

CONQUISTADORS

In Unit 6 you studied how European explorers discovered many new lands. In the fifteenth and sixteenth centuries, many European countries established colonies in various parts of the world, especially in those areas which are now known as the Americas. Here, Spanish and Portuguese explorers were followed by **Conquistadors** (Conquerors). They discovered ancient but advanced civilisations such as the **Aztecs** of Mexico and the **Incas** of Peru. These colonies in South America had huge quantities of gold and silver which were sent back to Europe in treasure ships. You have already studied Sir Francis Drake who hunted these ships in order to steal their cargo.

> **COLONY: a settlement in a new country, forming a community which is either partly or fully subject to the mother state.**

An artist's impression of European explorers arriving in the New World.

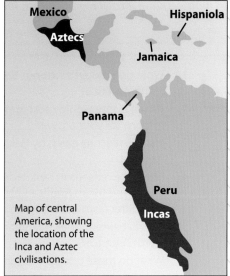

Map of central America, showing the location of the Inca and Aztec civilisations.

MI
TPD

RESEARCH

Find out more about the Aztecs and Incas. Make a list of bullet points about each civilisation.

Try to find at least six points about each one.

ENGLISH AMBITION

Many English people believed that they too should seek colonies in North America.

Below are some extracts from an English writer.

Richard Hakluyt was an English writer who lived from about 1552 to 1616. He was well educated, and, as well as being a Church of England minister, was also secretary to the English ambassador to France. He wrote a set of books called *Principal Navigations, Voyages and Discoveries of the English Nation* which set out a history of English explorations to date. In later life he became a strong supporter of the idea of establishing an English colony in North America.

If our nation were once planted in North America, or near thereabouts; whereas (English fishing boats) now fish but for two months of the year, they might then fish so long as pleased themselves.

... it is well known that all Savages ... as soon as they shall begin but a little to taste of civility, will take marvellous delight in any garment, be it never so simple; as a shirt, a blue, yellow, red or green cotton cassock, a cap, or such like, and will take incredible pains for such a trifle ... how great benefit to all Clothiers, Woolmen, Carders, Spinners, Weavers, Fullers etc would be the establishment of colonies in America and Far East.

... this voyage is not altogether undertaken for ourselves but ... the Savages shall have cause to bless the hour when this enterprise was undertaken.

First and Chiefly, in respect of the most happy and gladsome tidings of the most glorious gospel of our Saviour, Jesus Christ, whereby they may be brought from falsehood to truth ...

... being brought from brutish ignorance to civility and knowledge, they may be taught how one tenth of their land, if manured and ploughed, would yield as much as the whole presently does ...

But this is not all the benefit which they shall receive: for over and beside the knowledge how to till and dress their grounds, they shall be reduced from unseemly customs to honest manners, from disordered riotous routs to a well governed Commonwealth ...

It will prove a general benefit unto our country that, not only a great number of men which do now live idly at home and are a burden, chargeable and unprofitable to this realm, shall hereby be set to work, but also children of twelve and fourteen years of age or older, may be kept from idleness, in making of a thousand kinds of trifling things which will be good merchandise for that country and, moreover, our idle women shall also be employed on plucking, drying, and sorting of feathers, in pulling, beating and working of hemp, and in gathering of cotton, and diverse things for dyeing.

Extracts from *Principal Navigations*, Richard Hakluyt, 1598-1600

1. What do Hakluyt's writings tell you about the English view of the natives of North America?
2. Which quote would most appeal to an English wool merchant? Give reasons for your answer.
3. List the reasons given by Hakluyt for England to have colonies in North America.
4. List these reasons in rank order from the point of view of (a) a merchant/ trader and (b) an Anglican bishop. Suggest reasons why the rank orders may differ from each other.
5. To what extent does Hakluyt consider the best interests of the natives of North America?
6. What do these quotes this tell us about the author, Hakluyt?

ACTIVITY

Class Debate

Divide the class in two. One side will argue that England should set up colonies in North America. The other side will argue that they should not. Each side should give as many reasons as they can think of. At the end of the debate hold a vote to decide whose argument was stronger.

In 1585 the English made their first attempt to set up a colony in North America. It was on the east coast in what is now North Carolina, and was named **Roanoke**. They published a list of the reasons for establishing the colony:

1. To bring Christianity to the native people who were already living in the colony.
2. To enlarge the lands owned by the mother country.
3. To discover new lands and so learn more about the world.
4. To obtain goods at a cheaper price.
5. To act as naval bases from where ships could be supplied.
6. To provide employment for young people from the Mother Country.
7. By obtaining cheaper goods they would not have to rely on nations that were not their true friends.

The Native Americans who lived in this area were called the **Algonquin**. John White, the leader of the colony, made friends with them and made paintings which recorded their way of life. The Algonquin showed the colonists how to plant maize. They exchanged animal skins for glasses, knives and cooking pots. Two Algonquin even went back to England to meet Elizabeth I.

ACTIVITY

The first English baby to be born in the New World was Virginia Dare, the grandchild of John White. Here is a drawing of her baptism, made in 1880. Study it carefully and say what it might tell us about life in Roanoke.

Do you think this is a trustworthy source for an historian? Why or why not?

Peace did not last very long. One hundred soldiers came to Roanoke. They built a fort and started to take over the land, forcing the Algonquin to give them maize. When the Natives refused, quarrels developed and soon fighting broke out.

John White had left the colonists in 1587 and returned to England to get more supplies. However, England was fighting Spain and the Armada attack took place in 1588, so he was unable to get money to get supplies and return until 1590. On the next two pages is part of his story, telling what he found upon his return to Roanoke Island (the language has been modernised). Read the story carefully and answer the questions that follow.

… Our boats and all things fitted again, we put off from Hatorask, [modern day Hatteras in North Carolina] with a total of 19 persons in both boats. But before we could get to the place where the settlers had been left, it was so exceedingly dark that we overshot the place a quarter of a mile. There we saw, towards the north end of the island, the light of a fire through the woods, to which we rowed. When we came right over against it, we let fall our anchor near the shore, and sounded a trumpet call, and afterwards played many familiar English tunes, and called to them in a friendly manner, but we had no answer. We therefore landed at daybreak and, coming to the fire, we found the grass and various rotten trees burning about the place.

… we went through the woods … until we came to the place where I had left our colony in the year 1586. In all this way we saw in the sand footprints of two or three savages trodden during the night, and as we walked up the sandy bank we saw a tree, on the trunk of which were curiously carved these clear letters: C R O. We soon knew that these letters signified the place where I should find the settlers, according to a secret token agreed upon between them and me at my last departure from them, which was, that whatever happened they should write or carve on the trees or posts of the doors the name of the place where they were; for as I was leaving they were prepared to move from Roanoke to a place 50 miles away. Therefore at my departure from them in 1587 I instructed them, that if they should happen to be in trouble in any of those places, then they should carve over the letters or name, a cross. But we found no such sign of distress.

… we walked toward the place where we had left them in their houses, but we found the houses dismantled, and the place very strongly enclosed with a high palisade of large trees … very fort-like, and one of the biggest trees or posts at the right side of the entrance had the bark taken off, and five feet from the ground in fair capital letters was carved the word CROATOAN without any cross or sign of distress.

Having done this, we entered the palisade, where we found many bars of iron, two lumps of lead, four iron fowlers, iron sacker-shot, and other heavy items thrown here and there, almost overgrown with grass and weeds. [Later] we found five chests that had been carefully hidden by the settlers… three were my own, and … many of my things were damaged and broken, and my books torn from the covers, the frames of some of my pictures and maps rotten and spoiled with rain, and my armour almost eaten through with rust.

This could be no other but the deed … of our [native American] enemies at Dasamongwepeuk, who had watched the departure of our men to Croatoan, and as soon as they had departed, dug up every place where they suspected anything to be buried. But although it much grieved me to see such damage to my goods, yet on the other hand I greatly rejoiced that I had safely found a certain sign of their being safely at Croatoan, which is the place where Manteo [a friendly native American chief] was born, and the savages of the island our friends.

The next morning it was agreed by the Captain and myself, with the Master and others, to weigh anchor, and go to Croatoan, where our settlers were, for the wind was blowing in the right direction for that place, and also to leave our cask with fresh water on shore on the island until our return...

Account by John White, quoted in *"The Principal Navigations, Voyages, Traffiques, and Discoveries of the English Nation"*, Richard Hakluyt, 1590

However weather prevented them getting to Croatoan, and in the end they were forced to leave. It was not for another twelve years that another expedition was mounted, but it failed to even reach the area. The colonists were never seen again, and even today nobody knows what happened to them.

1. Why did White find it difficult to find the colony?
2. How did he try to contact the people there before he landed?
3. Who do you think had been at the campfire the previous evening? Give a reason for your answer.
4. When White arrived at the colony what was carved into the tree?
5. Explain why John White did not believe the colonists had been killed.
6. Do you think the colonists kept their promise to look after John White's possessions? Explain your answer.
7. Where did John White believe the colonists had gone?
8. What can we conclude from John White's use of the word "savages"?
9. Did you find any parts of John White's account hard to understand? If so, discuss them in class until you think you know what he meant. Write down any words that you didn't understand and find out what they mean.

UNIT 17: THE AMERICAN COLONIES

JAMESTOWN IS FOUNDED

ACTIVITY

In pairs, make a list of all the things that are needed to survive in a strange and possibly hostile place. Put these in the order you think is most important for survival. To do this, think of the consequences of *not* meeting a particular need. Compare your order with others in the class. If there are differences, try to persuade the class that your choices are the right ones.

In 1606, the English King, James I, granted permission to the London Virginia Company to take control of a large area of land in **Virginia**. They hoped to discover gold and silver there. The colonists sailed in three ships: *Discovery*, *Susan Constant*, and *God Speed*. They reached Chesapeake Bay in April 1607 and saw meadows, trees, and fresh waters, and met some Indians who seemed friendly. The first thing the new settlers did was to choose a site for their colony, something which the Company had given specific instructions about. Although **Jamestown**, which the colonists built, did not fulfill all the requirements, it was the best site they could find. They built a fort so that they would be safe if attacked. The next tasks were to clear the ground in order to make temporary houses for themselves, to plant vegetables, and to make nets for catching their food. They also had to start filling the ships with a cargo to take home, because the Company wanted its profit.

Location of the modern state of Virginia in the USA.

Artist's impression of the Jamestown colony

  Why do you think the English wanted to try to set up a colony in North America again, after what had happened to Roanoke?

JOHN SMITH

Before leaving England, the names of those chosen by the London Virginia Company to govern the colony were put in a locked box. This was opened when they reached America, and one of the seven names was John Smith, an army captain. However, he had quarreled so much with the others that the others refused to make him a council member. However in May, when the colony was only a month old, the native Indians raided the colony, and Smith was asked to help the colonists defend Jamestown.

Smith believed that the colonists needed to be made to work, and he took command. He famously said, "*If you do not work, you shall not eat*". This is what he later wrote about himself:

> *... by his own example, good words, and fair promises set some to mow, others to bind thatch; some to build houses, others to thatch them; himself always bearing the greatest task for his own share; so that, in short time, he provided most of them lodgings, neglecting any for himself.*

ACTIVITY

You are John Smith and you have to help to set up the colony in Jamestown, Virginia in 1607. Create a mind map of all that you will have to consider. You might start like this:

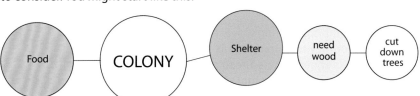

By September 1607 half of the original 104 settlers were dead from malaria or typhoid. As those who survived were very weak, it was even more necessary to build defences, as John Smith later wrote:

> *There were never Englishmen left in a foreign country in such misery as we were in this new discovered Virginia. We watched every three nights, lying on the bare cold ground, what weather so ever came; warded (guarded) all the next day; which brought our men to be most feeble wretches, not having five able men to man our bulwarks (strong defences) upon any occasion.*

The most pressing problem was shortage of food. Until they could grow their own crops, they had to trade with the Indians. They gave the Indians beads, copper and hatchets in return for bread, venison, turkeys and wild fowl. On one of these expeditions Smith is said to have been captured by some Indians who decided to kill him by beating his head with stones. Smith later wrote what happened next:

Pocahontas

> *Pocahontas, the King's dearest daughter, when no entreaty could prevail, got his head in her arms, and laid her own upon his to save him from death: whereat the King was contented he should live to make him hatchets, and her bells, beads and copper; for they thought him as well of all other occupations as them-selves, for the King himself will make his own robes, shoes, bows, arrows, pots.*

ACTIVITY

You are a reporter for a local radio news programme. You have to write a script for a short feature on the capture and near death of John Smith. You travel to Jamestown after Smith has safely returned, to interview both him and Pocahontas. You must include your own commentary and also excerpts from the interviews. You can interview others also, if you wish. Remember that this is for a **radio** programme, so you will not be able to use any pictures to help your listeners. If you present your feature to the class, you must do so from behind a curtain or screen so that your listeners cannot see you.

Afterwards, discuss this task. Did the class feel that your report was interesting and informative? Did you find it difficult? If so, what did you find difficult? What did you enjoy most about it?

Pocahontas later married an Englishman called John Rolfe. She came to England with him but died in 1617, aged only 22.

ACTIVITY

In 1616, Pocahontas is preparing to leave her country and people to make a dangerous sea journey to a strange land, England. Write a monologue in which Pocahontas thinks about what is ahead of her and how she feels about it. These are her thoughts so you can use more informal language.

ACTIVITY

Write a short obituary of Pocahontas for an English national newspaper.

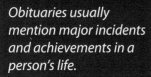

Obituaries usually mention major incidents and achievements in a person's life.

Smith returned to his colony and was made President on 10 September 1608. He extended the fort, tightened the discipline of the colonists and trained military units. Cargo was still being sent to England. In England, merchants were looking for pitch, tar, soap-ashes and cut wood and Smith was bitter because these things were not abundant in Virginia, where the colonists were struggling to live. The colonists had become very disgruntled, but Smith kept them together, mainly because they were impressed by his strong personality and achievements.

In July 1609 a ship left England carrying vital supplies, but also letters criticising Smith for not sending back enough goods. Smith returned to England and a new governor from London took over.

The colony grew gradually, but Indian massacres in 1622 and 1644 affected the flow of settlers. Eventually, the better weapons of the colonists defeated the Indians. A new town was built further inland, away from the unhealthy swamps, and great plantations developed using African slaves.

ACTIVITY

Class discussion

"John Smith had the personality and skills to be a good leader." Do you agree?

Start your discussion by considering what characteristics a good leader should have.

UNIT 18: IRELAND AND EARLY PLANTATIONS

ENGLISH CONTROL GROWS

Until the middle of the sixteenth century, the English could extend their control only over the part of Ireland around Dublin, known as **The Pale**. Areas outside this area were effectively independent, and paid little attention to English rule. The English King was represented in Ireland by a viceroy called the Lord Deputy.

The English faced many problems in Ireland, but from the middle of the sixteenth century they gradually extended their control over Ireland. One method which they used was the setting up of **plantations**, where English and Scottish **planters**, or settlers, came to live and work in Ireland. Early plantation schemes were carried out in counties Laois and Offaly (1556) Ards, in county Down (1570), county Antrim (1573) and in Munster (1586). The Irish resisted the English, and there was always the likelihood of trouble in Ireland in spite of English attempts to control the area.

RESEARCH

Pick one of the plantations named above and find out more about it. Try to find at least six interesting facts.

Present your findings using PowerPoint or similar software.

VICEROY: Someone with the right to speak on behalf of the King

Often people today describe something being "beyond the Pale". This phrase originated as a description of the areas of Ireland outside English control.

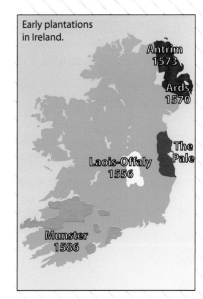

Early plantations in Ireland.

Here are some of the reasons why the English carried out plantations:
- The Irish chiefs had looked to Spain for help during a rebellion against English expansion led by the Earl of Desmond in Munster.
- The English feared that Spain might attack them via Ireland.
- There was a view that a barbaric country must first be broken by war before it will be capable of good government.
- The Irish remained Catholic, culturally Gaelic and used their own laws. England was not happy with this.
- The only area ruled directly by the English was The Pale. The English wanted to have more than just a foothold in Ireland.
- Henry VIII, the Protestant King of England, had taken the title 'King of Ireland'. Tudor governments therefore tried to make all of Ireland obey English law.

1. Which of the reasons for plantation address each of these statements:
   (a) "England is worried about foreign enemies."
   (b) "Religious differences are a problem."
   (c) "England wants to extend its control over Ireland."
2. Which of the reasons do you think was the most important? Give reasons for your answer.
3. What do you think Irish people at the time would have thought of each of the six reasons? Explain your answer.

THE NINE YEARS' WAR

After 1594 some of the most important Irish clans had gone to war against the forces of Queen Elizabeth I. They were led by **Hugh O'Neill** who was also known as the **Earl of Tyrone** and Hugh O'Donnell, the **Earl of Tyrconnell** (modern Donegal). The Irish claimed that they were fighting to preserve their old way of life which was being threatened by the expansion of English rule. This 'old way of life' meant the Irish system of culture and laws and the Roman Catholic faith. For some years they were successful, but on 24 December 1601 the Irish forces, reinforced by Spanish soldiers, were defeated at the Battle of Kinsale. Although O'Neill went back to Tyrone with his army, he now knew that he had little chance of winning against the English.

Hugh O'Neill, on the left, coming to parley with the English Commander before battle.

During 1602 the English strengthened their forts around O'Neill's territory in Tyrone. The Lord Deputy, Baron Mountjoy, ordered crops and cattle to be destroyed so the Irish would be starved into submission.

In the same year, one of O'Neill's allies, the head of the O'Cahan clan, made peace with the English, but despite this setback O'Neill still refused to surrender, and the English themselves decided to make peace because the war had proved very costly. The **Treaty of Mellifont** was signed in 1603. O'Neill gave up his Irish title and accepted English rule and laws and in return he was allowed to keep his lands.

Many of the English who had fought in Ulster saw how prosperous a land it could be and they were prepared to take the chance to live there.

> **PARLEY:** to discuss terms with an enemy.

Queen Elizabeth I died six days before the Treaty of Mellifont was signed. When O'Neill signed the Treaty he had not heard this news.

Do you think this knowledge might have affected his decision to sign? Why or why not?

ACTIVITY

Form groups. Compose a speech to be delivered to the English Parliament after the Treaty of Mellifont. Half of the groups have to argue for the benefits of English plantations in Ireland. The other half have to argue that plantations are not worth carrying out. Then, based on the two sets of speeches, the whole class has to vote on whether the Parliament should approve further plantations.

THE FLIGHT OF THE EARLS

When Elizabeth died in 1603 she was succeeded by her nearest relative, the son of Mary Queen of Scots, James VI of Scotland. James VI then became James I of England.

James I allowed O'Neill to remain the Earl of Tyrone and Hugh O'Donnell's brother Rory the Earl of Tyrconnell, but without any real power the Earls found it impossible to reconcile themselves to the new order. So, on the 14th September

1607, they gave up the struggle and left Ireland for Spain. They may have hoped to muster support and make a quick return to liberate Ireland, but we do not know. This departure from the shores of Lough Swilly at Rathmullan became known as the **Flight of the Earls**.

Towards the end of August 1607 a vessel steered into Lough Swilly and cast anchor off Rathmullan. Though it looked like a fishing boat, complete with fishing nets and salt, the ship had actually come with a messenger from the King of Spain, who went ashore with gifts of gold and silver. Hugh O'Neill was in Meath when the news of the vessel's arrival came to him. He quickly returned to his castle in Dungannon and then travelled all night with his family over the Sperrin mountains to Rathmullan. About a hundred people, "the cream of the Gaelic aristocracy" of Ulster, sailed away.

An artist's impression of the Flight of the Earls.

ACTIVITY

Discuss the picture of the Flight of the Earls. What is each person doing? Why might they be doing these things? What do you think the man with green sleeves is feeling? List as many things as you can think of.

The Earls never got to Spain. Storms at sea blew them instead onto the French coast. The French King, unwilling to offend the English King refused them permission to travel through France to Spain. Instead he sent them to the Spanish Netherlands. Their journey through Belgium, then south through Switzerland and Italy eventually took them to Rome where they arrived, a very tired and depleted party, on 29th April 1608.

Rory O'Donnell died in Rome the following year. Hugh O'Neill spent the rest of his life there and never ceased writing to the Spanish King urging him to send an army to Ireland. But by then the political atmosphere had changed in Europe and O'Neill's requests were ignored. O'Neill died in Rome in 1616.

Once settlers arrived from England and Scotland after 1609, O'Neill and O'Donnell's land of Ulster would become the stronghold of English control in Ireland.

> **LIBERATE:** to free from something
> **DEPLETED:** made less, reduced

 Do you think the Earls would have left Ireland if they had known how their story would end?

ACTIVITY

Imagine you are one of O'Neill's Irish soldiers who survived the defeat at the Battle of Kinsale. You have just heard the news that O'Neill has fled in the Flight of the Earls. Write a letter home to your family explaining how you feel about the English, how you felt about O'Neill before the Flight, and how you feel about him now. Also write about your hopes or fears for the future.

UNIT 19: THE ULSTER PLANTATION

PLANNING THE PLANTATION

VULNERABLE: easy to attack

The Nine Years' War had again shown the English just how vulnerable they could be to attack from Ireland, especially from the 'rebel' province of Ulster. This was especially worrying as the Spanish were keen to get revenge for the defeat of their famous Armada.

Many believed that Spain could use Ireland as a possible base from which to attack England. For this reason it became very important for the English to find a way to control Ulster.

TPD

Q Look at the general reasons for plantation given in Unit 18. Which of these was the main reason for planting Ulster?

Officials in London believed that as long as Catholics held land, they could raise the men and equipment necessary to stage another rebellion. Consequently, the English decided to plant colonies with Protestants, who would be loyal to the crown, giving them land and support to help them survive.

In 1609 a number of commissioners travelled Ulster, mapping the land and finding out who the owners were. They also found out which land belonged to the Church, because it was not to be confiscated. If people could not prove their ownership of land, it was usually taken from them.

About 4 million acres were involved in the scheme, but much of this was not very good land.

MA

Q
1. There are 0.4 acres in a hectare. How many hectares of land were involved in the scheme?
2. The total area of Ulster is about 5.3 million acres. What percentage of Ulster was involved in the scheme?

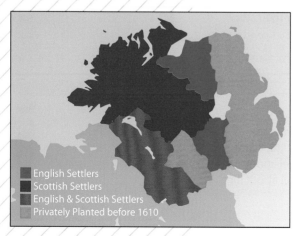

English Settlers
Scottish Settlers
English & Scottish Settlers
Privately Planted before 1610

The Province of Ulster, showing the counties planted in 1610.

Some lessons had been learned from earlier plantations. Settlers were not to live in scattered houses, but in fortified villages and towns.

A number of new towns were built by the settlers. A group of merchants called the 'London Companies' founded a city near the town of Derry, which they named **Londonderry**. You will learn more about this in the next unit. One of the men who was in charge of the plantation was Sir Arthur Chichester.

ACTIVITY

Here are some examples of plantation towns in Ulster: Coleraine, Cookstown, Derry/Londonderry, Letterkenny, Newtownards, Omagh. Look at a street map of one or more of these towns, or another plantation town you know, as it is today. See if you can trace the town centre and the road or street patterns there. Do you notice any pattern in the streets? If so, is the pattern different in the newer parts of the town (further from the centre)? Why do you think the towns have the pattern you can see?

These were the aims of the Ulster Plantation, according to Thomas Blenerhasset, who lived at the time of the plantation:

> 1. *The securing of that wild Country to the Crown of England.*
> 2. *The withdrawing of all the charge of the Garrison and men of war.*
> 3. *The rewarding of the old servitors to their good content.*
> 4. *The means how to increase the revenue to the Crown with a yearly very great sum.*
> 5. *To establish the Purity of Religion there.*
> 6. *And how the undertakers may with security be enriched.*
>
> *A Direction for the Plantation in Ulster* by Thomas Blenerhasset, Fermanagh, 1610

ACTIVITY

Discuss each of these points. What do you think each one means?

The English needed to carry out particular tasks in order to achieve these aims. These included:

1. Developing ports to expand trade.
2. Founding a series of new towns throughout Ulster.
3. Bringing in English and Scottish planters to settle the land.
4. Moving Catholic populations to poorest land in each region, and make the former land owners into tenants or labourers.
5. English soldiers and government officials would be offered cheap land.
6. Develop enough English/Scottish people and loyal Irish to end the threat of rebellion.

ATTRACTING SETTLERS

People who lived in England and Scotland were encouraged to start a life in the plantation. This is what Blenerhasset wrote to these people:

> *Art thou a tradesman, a smith, a weaver? Go to Ireland. Thou shall be higher in estimation and quickly enriched.*
>
> *Art thou a (farmer) whose worth is not past ten or twenty pounds? Go thither. Thou shall whistle sweetly and feed thy whole family if they be six, for sixpence a day.*
>
> *Art thou a minister of God's word? Make speed ... Thou shalt there see the poor ignorant untaught people worship stones and sticks. Thou, by carrying millions to heaven, may be made an archangel.*
>
> *A Direction for the Plantation in Ulster* by Thomas Blenerhasset, Fermanagh, 1610

ACTIVITY

Design a brochure or make a short video to be given to people in England and Scotland to explain why coming to Ireland to settle would be a good idea. Think carefully about all the information you should give and use persuasive language.

ACTIVITY

Class discussion

How do you think the native Irish would have felt about the Plantation? What would have happened to a Catholic Irish farmer who owned some good land in Ulster? What would he have thought of what Blenerhasset wrote, telling people to "go to Ireland"?

> **UNDERTAKER:** In the plantation, somebody who was granted land
>
> **BAWN:** A defensive wall round a house

Several different groups of people benefitted from the Plantation, and most of those who were granted land had to obey specific rules:

English and Scottish undertakers

- undertook to bring only English and Scottish tenants;
- to build fortifications according to land granted:

  for 1,000 acres they had to build a **bawn**, and for 1,500 acres or more they had to build a bawn and a castle.
- tenants to live near bawns and keep arms in readiness.

Servitors (solders who had served in the Nine Years' War)

- had served the crown in Ireland;
- could have Irish tenants;
- had to make the same fortifications as the undertakers.

Loyal Irish (who had not rebelled in the War)

- received a tenth of the plantation land;
- same terms as Servitors;
- must use English farming methods.

Guilds

- mainly from London and had been involved in Virginia plantations.
- The Irish Society was established to look after County Londonderry for them as they were usually absentees.

Others

- The Protestant Church of Ireland received all former Catholic church land.
- Five free schools were established to educate the sons of merchants and plantation farmers. These **Royal Schools** were sited in Dungannon, Enniskillen, Cavan, Raphoe and Armagh.

ACTIVITY

Using the information above, produce a mind map giving details of the plantation grants. Start like this:

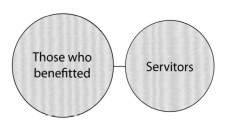

Those who benefitted

Servitors

A replica plantation bawn at the former Ulster History Park near Omagh.

ACTIVITY

You have now studied examples of colonisation in both America and Ireland.

Form a committee to plan a new colony in a newly discovered country in the seventeenth century.

What plans would you make with reference to religion, social requirements and establishing a political system? What would be the first problem you might face? How would you treat the people who lived there before you? How would you deal with the different language of the indigenous population?

Draw up a 10 point constitution to establish the initial standards you will expect from settlers and natives.

INDIGENOUS: native

UNIT 20: THE LONDON COMPANIES
CASE STUDY

FOUNDING THE CITY

In the previous unit you learned that county Londonderry was settled by the London Companies. These were **guilds** or **trade associations**, each of which regulated a trade such as drapery or fishmongers. You had to be a member of a guild to set up business in that trade, but you could then get help from other members if you were in trouble. They set up an organisation called The Irish Society to carry out the work. They founded the town of Coleraine and a new city close to the Irish settlement of Derry, which they named **Londonderry**. Work on the city began in 1613 and the walls were completed in 1618. Because the city was planned, the streets were laid out in a pattern that can still be seen today. In 1633 the Church of Ireland Cathedral of St Columb was completed. Both the cathedral and the walls survive to this day.

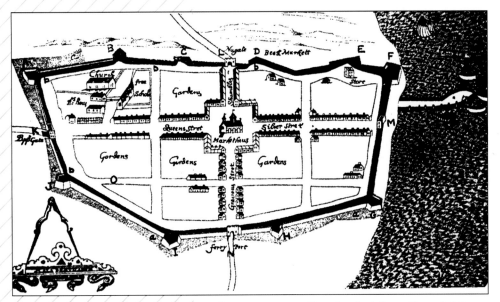

Contemporary map of how the plantation settlement at Derry looked in 1625

The seventeenth century city walls remain almost intact to the present day.

 Look at the picture of the walls today. What might the turreted structure built into the wall have been?

 Why do you think the London companies added the word 'London' to the word 'Derry'? What were the benefits of doing so? What problems did it create?

ACTIVITY

Find out more about the site of the walled city of Londonderry. Consider these questions:

1. What advantages did this site offer to persuade the Irish Society to site their new city here?

2. Why do you think they built the city walls before they built the cathedral?

When you think you know the answers to these questions, write a short speech that you have to deliver to the head of the Irish Society in 1612. You must persuade him that you have found the perfect site for a fortified settlement. You must also give a reason for the importance of building the walls first. Perhaps you will be chosen to give your speech to the class!

ACTIVITY

The Northern Ireland Tourist Agency have commissioned a new web site to tell people about the history of Northern Ireland. You have been asked to compose a section on the history and remains of the walls of Derry. Make a plan of the web page you will write, deciding on sections and headings. Then word process your contribution in your own words. Make into hyperlinks any words which might usefully be links to other parts of the web site.

PLANTING THE COUNTY

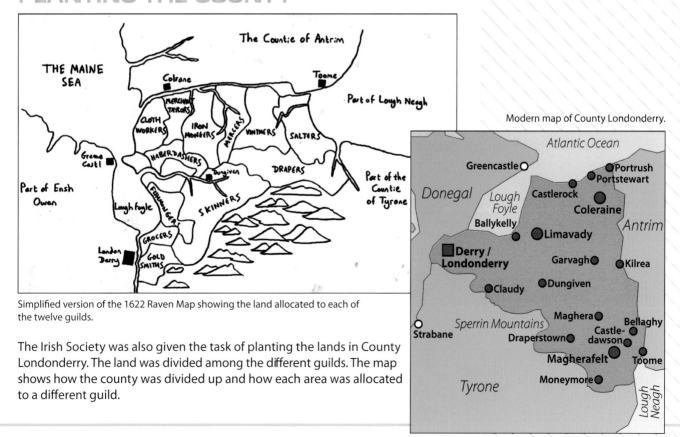

Simplified version of the 1622 Raven Map showing the land allocated to each of the twelve guilds.

Modern map of County Londonderry.

The Irish Society was also given the task of planting the lands in County Londonderry. The land was divided among the different guilds. The map shows how the county was divided up and how each area was allocated to a different guild.

Look at the modern map of County Londonderry.

1. Can you see a town that is named after the guild that planted the surrounding land?

2. Below is a list of modern towns, and the names of some guilds. Match each town to the guild that settled the land the town is in:

Kilrea	Magherafelt	Drapers	Salters
Bellaghy	Moneymore	Mercers	Vintners
Dungiven		Skinners	

In what ways is the 1622 map different from a modern map?

TPD

You have already seen that individual planters had to build a bawn and possibly a castle if they had a lot of land. What other things would the London Companies have had to build in order to manage the settlement of an entire county?

The Guilds

The shield of the guild of fishmongers.

Twelve guilds were involved in planting County Londonderry. Some date back to the eleventh century, and many of them survive to the present day, although they have less of a role in controlling trades now. Each guild has a shield which has a picture that represents what trade the guild is responsible for.

ACTIVITY

Some of the London guilds have obvious names. But others are less obvious. Find out what trade each of the following guilds controlled:

Mercers	Skinners	Haberdashers	Drapers
Vintners	Cutlers	Salters	Farriers

MI
TPD

TPD

What trade do you think this shield represented? Give reasons for your answer.

BC
SM

 ACTIVITY

Design your own shield demonstrating information about yourself, your hobbies, your ambitions and your skills.

EARLY DAYS

Omagh was founded during the Ulster Plantation. It was the place where Hugh O'Neill fought one of his last battles with Lord Mountjoy at the end of the Nine Years' War. This is what Sir Arthur Chichester, one of the leaders of the Ulster Plantation, said about this part of Tyrone in 1602:

> *Round this place there is great desolation, by reason of which it happeneth that merchants and other passengers weekly guarded travelling from Derrie or Liffer to the Pale are usually in their passage cut off and murdered.*

In 1609 the district and new town was granted to Lord Castlehaven, but he failed to erect a castle and settle the proper number of English on the land as was required by the grant. This was not the only place where Lord Castlehaven had failed to fulfil the terms of a plantation grant. This is what was written about his plantation grant in Forkhill, in south County Armagh:

> *The Earl of Castlehaven hath 3,000 acres. Upon this there is no building at all, either of Bawns or Castle ... I find planted on this land some few English families ... [who] since the old Earl died, (as they tell me) cannot have [land] unless, they will bring treble the rent which they paid; and yet they ... have but half the land which they enjoyed in the old Earl's time ...*
>
> *The Earl hath more 2,000 acres ... Upon this there was a large house begun, but it is pulled down and made but half so great ... The agent for the Earl showed me the Rent-Roll of all the Tenants ... but they are all leaving the land. The rest of the land is let to 20 Irish Gentlemen ... and these Irish Gentlemen have under them about 3,000 souls of all sorts.*
>
> A description of Lord Castlehaven's estate at Forkhill. From *Pynnar's Survey*, written 1619

1. How had Lord Castlehaven failed his undertaking?
2. Sir Arthur Chichester's description does not give a good impression of the town, so why do you think people were still prepared to take grants of land in this area from the crown?

THE TOWN IS BUILT

As a result, the land around Omagh reverted to the crown and was then granted to Captain Edmund Leigh and his brothers John and Daniel. By 1611 Omagh seems to be well improved, judging by this description by Lord Carew who was sent to review the progress of the plantation:

> *The Fort of Omye. Here is a good fort fairly walled with lime and stone about thirty feet high above the ground with a parapet, the river on one side and a large deep ditch about the rest; in which is built a fair house of timber after the English manner. Begun by Captain Edmund Leigh and finished by his brothers, at their own change, upon the lands of the Abbey of Omye, at which place are many families of English and Irish, who have built them good dwelling houses, which is a safety and comfort for passengers between Dungannon and the Liffer. The fort is a place of good import upon all occasions of service and fit to be maintained.*
>
> Lord Carew, writing in 1611.

ACTIVITY

Plan of Action

Edward, John and Daniel Leigh seem to have improved the settlement at Omagh within two years between 1609 and 1611. Imagine you are Captain Edward Leigh and it is 1609. You have just visited the area and seen how bad things are. Devise a plan of action to bring the settlement up to a good standard. Keep in mind the requirements laid down by law. Start with an assessment of the situation. Then draw up a two-year plan of work.

ACTIVITY

Today Omagh has a road called 'Irishtown Road'. 'Irishtown' was the name given to areas where the native Irish were required to live. If you live in a town, choose two road or street names and find out how they got their names. If you live in the country, choose the names of two townlands and find out what they mean.

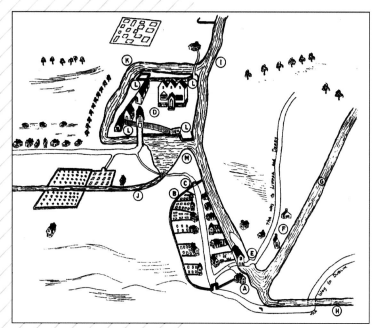

Map of Omagh in 1610. This is the oldest known map of the town.

The map shows the main features of the new town of Omagh:

A = Old castle (near modern Dublin Road / Market Street junction)

B = A cross

C = North gate

D = Bawn

E = Mill

F = Inn, for travellers

G = Camowen river

H = Drumragh river

I = Strule river

J = Brook

K = Moat

L = Gun emplacements

M = Gates to the basin (for boats)

1. In what ways is the bawn at Omagh similar to the bawn in Unit 19 (page 63)?
2. Who may have drawn the map of Omagh and for what reason?
3. What can we learn from the map about how secure the residents of Omagh felt?

ACTIVITY

Based on the map and the description by Lord Carew, write a tourist information leaflet telling people what Omagh is like in 1610/11. Describe how the town looks, what the main buildings are, where travellers might find accommodation and anything else that might be of interest to visitors.

ACTIVITY

Class discussion

What would it have been like to go and live in Omagh in 1610/11? What would be benefits of moving to the town, and what would have been the risks? Do you think life would have been easy or hard?

Later in 1631, Charles I granted the manor of Arleston or Audleston, of 2,000 acres of land in and around Omagh, to James Mervyn. Mervyn built three castles. There is now no trace of the castle at Ballynahatty. Of the other two, only the corners remain standing at Trillick and at Kirlish, near Drumquin.

COLONISATION
UNIT 22: RESULTS OF THE ULSTER PLANTATION

As expected, the Ulster Plantation changed the country quite dramatically. It did much to make this part of Ireland different from the rest of the country. The rebellious nature of the people was not quashed completely and there was, understandably, opposition to such English intrusion. There were four main results of the plantation:

1. settlement of many new people
2. opposition from the Irish
3. religious changes
4. introduction of a different way of life.

NEW SETTLERS

By 1622 perhaps 20,000 settlers had come to Ulster from England, and especially from Scotland. Although those who were given land grants were often from wealthy backgrounds, most of the settlers were ordinary people who decided to seek a better life in the plantation. There were both push and pull factors in people's decision to come:

Push Factors

1. The Government in Scotland were becoming more strict with criminals. Those with a criminal record found it harder to live there.
2. The population in Scotland was rising and this meant more competition for people renting farms and looking for work.
3. Landlords in Scotland offered only short term leases for farms and so farmers had to keep moving from farm to farm.

Pull Factors

1. Ulster was a place to escape and hide if you were wanted as a criminal.
2. Ulster was sparsely populated and there was plenty of space for new settlers.
3. Landlords offered longer leases for farms.
4. Ulster had good farmland for growing crops and grazing animals, more forest for timber and rivers and lakes with plenty of fish in them.

However, there were new economic problems that settlers had to face in Ulster. For example, they had to pay for lots of different things as well as their rent:

Tithe – tenants had to make a regular payment to the Church of Ireland. This was usually paid in kind, for example the produce of a day's work.

Lease – to secure a tenancy for a long period, eg 30 years, you had to make a payment over and above your normal rent payment.

Duty Day – each tenant had to work for the landlord on a certain number of days each year.

Taxes – which had to be paid to the King

Heriot – this was a special tax that was due on the death of a tenant. The tenant's widow had to give the landlord the best beast on the farm.

Hearth money – a property tax of 2 shillings for every hearth (or fireplace) in the house.

INTRUSION: unwanted entry

IN KIND: Exchanging labour or goods, instead of money, as payment

Look at the six payments opposite. From the point of view of the tenant, do you think each one is fair, or unfair? Explain your answer.

ACTIVITY

Form into two groups. Imagine you are all poor farmers working on rented land in Scotland. One group has to argue that they should leave Scotland and join the plantation in Ulster. The other group has to argue that it's not worth going to Ulster. At the end of the discussion hold a vote to decide whether to go to Ulster or stay in Scotland.

OPPOSITION

Although some of the native Irish were willing to pay rent to the newcomers rather than move from their land, many bitterly resented having to do so. They vowed to made life difficult for the planters. The planters should have expected trouble from the people whose land they were taking up. They had been encouraged, from the outset, to provide fortifications and to ensure that their tenants were armed against attack. After the bawns were built, life was more secure for the planters as the tenants could retreat behind the walls when threatened, but travellers were always in danger. When passing through wooded or mountainous country they were easy targets, as were those living in more isolated farms.

Monea Castle, a bawn in County Fermanagh, as it would have looked when new.

Monea Castle today.

Look at the drawing of Monea Castle in the seventeenth century and the photograph of the remains today. What part of the original building do you think you can see today?

DISPOSSESSED: someone who has had property forcibly taken away

Woodkern raiding a plantation settlement.

The main opposition came from the Irish swordsmen who were the armed followers of the dispossessed Irish chiefs. The government had sent some of them into exile but most of them escaped and lived rough in the woods and hills. These people were called woodkern.

They tried to stop the planters from building and often attacked their farms. This was one of the main reasons why it was so difficult to persuade English and Scottish tenants to settle on the land.

Look at the picture of the woodkern on a raid. Write down some adjectives that describe the mood of the picture. Do you think the artist was more sympathetic to the native Irish or the settlers? How can you tell? Do you think this is a reliable source for historians studying the life of the native Irish after the plantation? Explain your answer.

ACTIVITY

Imagine you are part of a band of woodkern. You have just returned to your camp after a raid. Write a diary entry describing why you think the raid was justified and what happened. Include details of what you took, and how you feel about the planters.

Because the prehistoric *Scotti* peoples had migrated from north-east Ireland to Scotland during the fifth century AD (giving Scotland its name), some people justified the Plantation by claiming that the planters were merely returning home to Ireland. This is what one historian later wrote:

> *When the Galloway [Scottish] planters came to Ulster they were only returning to their own lands like emigrants returning home again.*
>
> F J Biggar, writing circa 1900. Quoted by I Adamson in *The Identity of Ulster*, Pretani Press, 1982

How convincing is Biggar's argument that the planters were merely emigrants returning to their own lands? Explain your opinion.

RELIGIOUS CHANGES

Protestant reformers in Scotland followed the teachings of a preacher called John Calvin, rather than Martin Luther or the Church of England (Anglican). Their reformed church became known as the Church of Scotland, while Scots who followed Anglican ways became known as Episcopalians. In Ireland we use different names. Followers of John Calvin became known as Presbyterians, while the Anglican church here became known as the Church of Ireland.

RESEARCH

Find out more about the differences between the Presbyterian Church and the Church of Ireland. Study things like how they came to exist, what they believe, what their church buildings look like inside and how each was treated by the government during the time of the Penal Laws. Present your findings using PowerPoint or similar software.

Many of those who came to Ulster brought with them, from Scotland, their Presbyterian beliefs. The Presbyterian church permitted ordinary members to play an important part in governing their church. Many of these people would later become very active in Irish revolutionary politics claiming that they should be allowed a part in governing their country as well as their church.

However, not all Scots were regarded as a good influence. Here are the opinions of two people writing at the time:

> *From Scotland came many and from England not a few, yet all of them generally the scum of both nations who from debt or law breaking and fleeing from justice come hither ... most of these people ... cared little for any church ... with fighting, murder, adultery etc.*
>
> From *History of the Church of Ireland after the Scots were naturalised*, written 1670–71, by Andrew Stewart. Quoted by WD Killen, Belfast, 1866.

> *... the most part were such as either poverty, scandalous lives, or at the best adventurers seeking of better accommodation had forced thither ... the security and thriving of religion was little seen to by these adventurers and the preachers were generally ... the same.*
>
> From *The life of Mr Robert Blair*, written about 1663, by R Blair. Quoted by T McCrie, Edinburgh, 1848.

Also, not all planters were Protestant. The Bishop of Derry wrote to the Lord Chancellor in 1629:

> *Sir George Hamilton ... has done his best to plant Popery ... and has brought over priests ... from Scotland.*

A DIFFERENT WAY OF LIFE

PURITAN: A Protestant with very strict rules for living.

WORK ETHIC: The belief that hard work is a sign that you love God

These colonists brought to Ulster a way of life very different from the rest of the country. Many had brought modern farming methods and a tradition of the Puritan work ethic. In Ulster, as a result of the Plantation, both landlord and tenant were usually Protestant and both spoke English. In years to come, these differences would have major implications for relations between landlord and tenant in Ulster and the rest of the country.

Some Scots had settled in Ulster independently of the plantation scheme. The most important of these were Hugh Montgomery and James Hamilton from Ayrshire who settled in south Antrim and north Down. They were very successful. Both men had helped to get a royal pardon for an Irish Cheiftain, Conn O'Neill, in 1602 and in return had been granted parts of O'Neill's land.

However, the native Irish were never fully removed from the land and purely British settlements were not established. A rebellion in 1641 (see Unit 25) showed that the ability of the native Irish in Ulster to wage war was not destroyed by the plantation process, even though it was by then too firmly established to be totally overthrown.

ACTIVITY

Hot seat!

One person should sit at the front of the class and play the part of either (a) an Irish Catholic who has lost land or (b) an Irish Protestant landowner who was already in Ulster before the Plantation.

The rest of the class should ask him/her questions about how they feel and what they intend to do about their position.

ACTIVITY

You have been living in Ulster now for three years. Write a letter home to your friends telling them how you are getting on.

Choose the class of colonist you wish to be: Undertaker, Servitor or tenant (see Unit 19).

Include the reasons you left Scotland, why you chose to come to Ulster, what difficulties you found here and what success you can claim.

ACTIVITY

Class Discussion

Before you move on from this section, discuss how you think an historian might relate the events of the seventeenth century in Ireland, and in particular Ulster, to the history of the country as it developed later.

Review this Section

How do you regard the first colonists to America? Do you think they were very brave – or very foolish?

Would anyone in the class think they would like to be a first-generation colonist? If so, what would you like about the experience?

Can you think of any country or people today who want to set up a colony in another land? What modern motives might there be for colonisation? Could they be the same as in the seventeenth century?

Does anything you have learnt in this section help you to understand modern Ireland any better?

Word Check

Check out these words to make sure you can spell them.

Mellifont	Tyrconnell	navigation
discipline	Laois	community
Plantation	Offaly	incredible
Meath	secretary	Christianity
civilisation	Pocahontas	employment
hatchet	settler	language
Tyrone	Chesapeake	

If you're not sure if you can spell any of them, check them out a few more times.

END OF SECTION QUIZ

Class Quiz!

Divide into two teams and decide on a prize for the winning team. If you get a question right, your team gets a point, BUT if you get a question wrong, you lose a point! So think carefully before you answer.

1. Where and what was The Pale?

2. What was the name of the colony set up by the English in America in 1585?

3. Who did Pocahontas marry?

4. What was the name of the Society set up to look after the London Guilds' lands in Co Londonderry?

5. Who was the King or Queen after Elizabeth I?

6. From which two parts of the British Isles did most of the planters in Ireland come from?

7. From where did the Flight of the Earls take place?

8. The area that the Aztecs lived is in what modern country?

9. Name the four provinces of Ireland.

10. Name two things the English and Scottish undertakers had to agree to do in order to be granted land in Ireland.

11. Who was the first English baby to be born in the New World?

12. Who were the woodkerne?

13. Name three of the London Guilds that were given land around Derry.

14. What fatal diseases did the settlers in Jamestown suffer from?

15. What is the Spanish word for 'Conquerors'?

16. Who said, "If you do not work, you shall not eat", and where did he say it?

17. In what year was the colony of Jamestown founded?

18. What does 'to parley' mean?

19. Which Irish leader signed the Treaty of Mellifont with the English?

20. Name three Plantation towns in Ulster.

Before you start

Have a go at this research!

Draw four columns in your notebook.

- In the first column, make a list of ten countries in Europe. If you can't think of ten, use an atlas or search on the Internet.
- In the second column, write down whether the country is a monarchy or a republic.
- In the third column, for each republic, note down whether or not it used to be a monarchy. For each monarchy, note down whether it used to be a republic.
- In the fourth column, note down in what year it changed from monarchy to republic, or vice versa.

In which direction is the change more common – monarchy to republic or republic to monarchy? Discuss your findings.

You will learn in this Section that England went from a monarchy to a republic and back to a monarchy again!

JAMES I

James I of England (and VI of Scotland, reigned from 19 June 1566 – 27 March 1625) was married to Anne of Denmark. They had seven children but only three survived childhood.

James believed very strongly in the **Divine Right of Kings**. This meant that he believed absolutely that he had been chosen by God to be King and therefore ordinary people should not question what he said or did.

Do you remember who James' mother was?

How long was his reign, in years and months?

James had lots of opinions about people's lifestyles. He disliked the habit of tobacco smoking (which had been introduced from the newly discovered lands in America) very much and wrote a pamphlet in 1604 entitled *Counterblasts to Tobacco*, condemning this habit. Here is a quotation from it:

> *Have you not reason then to bee ashamed, and to forbeare this filthie noveltie, …? In your abuse thereof sinning against God, harming your selves both in persons and goods, … by the custome thereof making your selves to be wondered at by all forraine civil Nations, and by all strangers that come among you, to be scorned and contemned. A custome lothsome to the eye, hatefull to the Nose, harmefull to the braine, dangerous to the Lungs, and in the blacke stinking fume thereof, neerest resembling the horrible Stigian smoke of the pit that is bottomelesse.*

COM
TPD

ACTIVITY

Rewrite the extract from the pamphlet in modern English. Look up any words that you don't understand.

Under your new version, write a list of all the things James thinks is wrong with smoking.

METRICAL: a rhythmic structure, like poetry

Title page of the first King James Bible, 1611

James also had many concerns about religion in general. He commissioned an "**Authorised Version**" of the Bible in English. This version, sometimes still called the **King James Version**, came out in 1611.

He was also interested in converting the Psalms into metrical form so that they could be sung. He was doing this himself but died before they were published in 1631.

RELIGIOUS PROBLEMS

Both James I and his son Charles I faced opposition from various religious groups. The three main religious groups active in England at this time were:

Anglicans (Church of England):

The Anglican way of worship and the rule of bishops had become common during Elizabeth I's reign and the majority of the population wanted this to continue. James himself favoured the Anglicans and this angered the other two religious groups. The leading figure in the Anglican church was Archbishop Laud who was particularly opposed to the Puritans.

Puritans:

The Puritans were more extreme Protestants who favoured simple church services and a 'religious' lifestyle that emphasised the importance of Biblical teaching and moral purity.

Catholics:

The Catholics had retained their connection to the Pope in Rome during the Reformation, despite pressure from Protestants to convert.

A modern replica of the Mayflower

As James had been brought up by Puritan nobles in Scotland, the Puritans hoped for favours from the new King. When James I did not favour them, they were angry. A small group decided to leave England to found a new community in America. They were known as the **Pilgrim Fathers** and they sailed to America on the *Mayflower* in 1620. They were intending to go to Virginia but were blown off course and landed hundreds of miles to the north in present day Massachusetts where they founded a town called Plymouth. In the first years, friendly Indians helped the settlers:

A Puritan man and woman on their way to church.

> *[One Indian] was their interpreter and was sent from God for their good. He directed them how to set their corn, where to take fish and to gain other types of food and never left them until he died.*
>
> William Bradford, leader of the Plymouth colony.

How can we tell that the 'Indian' that William Bradford refers to had previously met Englishmen?

During the next few years thousands of Puritans made their way to the states on the east coast of America, looking for religious freedom. They also got cheap land and the chance of a fresh start in a new country.

RESEARCH

Every November, people in the USA celebrate the festival of *Thanksgiving*. Find out the connection between the Puritans and this festival. Why do Americans celebrate it today?

If you have time, you could divide into groups and make a collage about Thanksgiving. Display your collages in the classroom or on a school noticeboard.

Here are some of the things Puritans sailing to America were told to bring:

> *...the following tools for a family of six:*
> *4 hoes, 3 shovels and 2 spades, 2 broad axes,*
> *5 felling axes, 2 steel hand-saws, 2 two-hand saws,*
> *1 whipsaw with file and set 2 augers, 6 chisels,*
> *2 pickaxes, 1 grindstone, nails of all sorts.*
>
> Advice to pioneers published in England in 1622.

Why do you think people sailing to America were advised to bring these items? What would they have needed them for?

Catholics, too, had hoped for favours from James, because both his mother and his wife were Catholic, but James I ignored their demands once he became King of England and Ireland in 1603 (he was King of Scotland before this). As a result, a small number of Catholic nobles began plotting to kill the King, and this led to the **Gunpowder Plot** of 1605 which we will look at in the next unit.

ACTIVITY

From the point of view of (a) a Puritan and (b) a Roman Catholic, write two letters to James I in 1604, asking him to look favourably on your religion. Mention his background and why, because of this, you think he should favour your cause.

Suggest reasons why these letters would differ.

THE PLOT

When James VI of Scotland became King of England and Ireland in 1603 it soon became clear to leading Catholics in England that they could not expect protection from the new ruler. Therefore they decided to take over the government of England by force, by killing the King and the most important men in the country. The best time to do this was when they were all together at the state opening of Parliament. Their plan was to blow up Parliament on the 5 November 1605, and then put a new Catholic king on the throne.

> The Parliament building that was present at the time of the Gunpowder Plot was demolished in 1824. The Houses of Parliament that you can see in London today are actually relatively recent, completed around 1860.

James I of England / VI of Scotland.

It now appears very likely that some people close to the King knew of this plot and were prepared to let the plotters go far enough that they could be found guilty of treason and executed. The plotters rented a cellar beneath the Houses of Parliament. They did not take into account two things. Firstly, it was suspicious that it had been so easy to find and rent a cellar. Secondly, they did not realise just how damp such a cellar would be and the effect this would have on the gunpowder.

Picture from the time of the plot, showing the main conspirators.

The plotters stored 36 barrels of gunpowder, again fairly easily, in the cellar. They hid the gunpowder under a pile of firewood and laid a trail of it to the door. The plotters assumed once they lit it, it would take about 15 minutes until the explosion, giving them enough time to escape – but they never got a chance to light it.

The artist who drew this picture probably never met any of the people shown. How valuable is this as a source for historians studying the Gunpowder Plot?

THE MONTEAGLE LETTER

The plot failed because one of the plotters, Francis Tresham, tried to warn his brother-in-law, Lord Monteagle, to stay away from the state opening of Parliament. Tresham sent a very mysterious letter to Monteagle and it was shown to James I:

My Lord, out of the love I bear to some of your friends, I have a care of your preservation. Therefore I would advise you, as you tender your life, to devise some excuse to shift your attendance at this parliament; for God and man hath concurred to punish the wickedness of this time. And think not slightly of this advertisement, but retire yourself into your country where you may expect the event in safety. For though there be no appearance of any stir, yet I say they shall receive a terrible blow this Parliament; and yet they shall not see who hurts them. ... The danger is past as soon as you have burnt this letter.

Extract from Tresham's letter to Lord Monteagle, 1605.

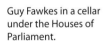

Guy Fawkes in a cellar under the Houses of Parliament.

The letter made the King suspicious and he ordered a search of the cellars of the House of Lords on 4 November. This led to the discovery and arrest of **Guy Fawkes** who, after being tortured in the Tower of London, confessed his role in the Gunpowder Plot.

Lord Monteagle's family was Catholic and he had been involved in a rebellion in 1601 against Queen Elizabeth I. However in 1605 he wrote to the King saying he had become a Protestant and Lord Monteagle was allowed to sit in the House of Lords.

He was rewarded by the King for helping to prevent the Plot. Guy Fawkes and the other conspirators were executed.

I will live and die in that religion which I have now resolved to profess.

Lord Monteagle, in a letter to James I in 1605.

Some historians suspect that Lord Monteagle knew about the plot, and that he actually faked the letter himself. What motivation could he have had to do this?

ACTIVITY

You are a TV news correspondent reporting live to camera on the State Opening of Parliament. You are waiting for the King and the beginning of the proceedings. You are just commenting to viewers that things seem to be running late when you hear a commotion and someone comes running past you shouting something about explosives.

Write a script for this scene and what follows and then perform it in class. Remember you are live on camera and there will be other people around you. For example, you might try to stop someone to interview them to find out what is going on. Use your imagination!

UNIT 25: CHARLES I AND PARLIAMENT

CHARLES I

When James I died, his son **Charles I** became King. Here are some facts about Charles:

- Born in 1600, second son of James VI of Scotland and Queen Anne.
- Elder brother Henry died in 1612.
- Often sick as a child, was bow-legged and had a stutter.
- Very deeply religious especially favouring Roman Catholicism.
- Loved paintings, especially Italian and Belgian art.
- Married a Catholic French princess, Henrietta Maria, with whom he had seven children.
- Believed in the divine right of kings, and that he had to answer only to God for his actions.

ACTIVITY

Re-write all the bullet points above to make a well constructed paragraph of text.

DEFIED: did not do as they were told

The English Parliament did not like Charles and refused to give him all the money he asked for.

There were two main reasons why Parliament defied the King:

Religion: Charles was sympathetic to the Roman Catholics, and his wife was a Catholic. He may have wished to ally England with Spain. Most members of Parliament were Protestant and many of these were strict Puritans.

Parliament wanted more power: Members of Parliament wanted regular elections and they didn't like the King raising taxes or making new laws without the consent of Parliament.

They disagreed with the idea that the King had to answer only to God and not to any earthly authority.

The King quarrelled so much with Parliament that in 1629 he dismissed it and ruled for 11 years on his own. This did not make him popular. By 1640 he had to recall Parliament as he was so short of money. During the next year Parliament consistently tried to limit the King's power. A small group led by **John Pym** started the campaign against the King's actions and were soon joined by almost every MP. Charles had to give in to their demands. Unpopular money raising schemes introduced by the King during the 1630s were made illegal.

The courts, which were unfair and sometimes used torture, were abolished.

A law was passed making sure Parliament would meet regularly.

The King's power was greatly reduced, and some of his key advisers, such as the Earl of Strafford and Archbishop Laud, were executed.

John Pym

IRELAND AND SCOTLAND

In 1641 many of the Catholics in Ireland, especially Ulster, who had lost their land as a result of the Plantation rebelled against the King. They were worried that the English Parliament was going to send an army into Ireland to try to get rid of Catholicism.

Can you think of any other reasons why Irish Catholics may have wanted to rebel?

The rebellion turned into a conflict between Irish Catholics and Protestant settlers. Most historians believe around 4000 Protestants were killed by Catholics, especially in one incident at Portadown. This is what one survivor wrote:

A picture drawn around 1645 showing the event in Portadown. The artist may or may not have been present at the event.

> *We were locked up, 100 men and children, in Loughgall church. Many were sore, tortured by strangling and half hanging... then driven like hogs six miles to the River Bann in Portadown ... pushed onto the bridge, stripped naked and then forced by pikes into the river... those that did not drown were shot at by the rebels as they tried to swim ashore... I was saved by paying a rebel £15. The leader of the rebels was Toole McCann.*

William Clarke, a survivor of the massacre at Portadown in 1641.

ACTIVITY

Compare the account of William Clarke and the picture of the events in Portadown. Is each one a primary or a secondary source? Do they support or contradict each other? How reliable is each one as a source for historians?

Later an army arrived in Ireland from Scotland. This resulted in more killings, this time of Catholics by Protestants. For example several hundred Catholics are said to have been killed on Rathlin Island by being thrown off cliffs.

In August 1641 Charles I travelled to Scotland to meet the leaders of a group who were opposed to Presbyterianism in Scotland and who disliked the English Parliament. Parliament was very suspicious of this, and wondered what Charles was up to. Then, in November 1641 Charles asked Parliament for money to raise an army to put down the Irish rebellion. Parliament suspected that Charles was actually going to use the army against them.

Do you think the events of 1641 in Ireland had anything to do with the dispute between the King and Parliament in England?

PATH TO CIVIL WAR

Charles I trying to arrest the five Members of Parliament.

Charles was so angry about Parliament's campaign against him that, in January 1642, he marched into the House of Commons to arrest the five MPs who had most annoyed him. They escaped, but this action marked the beginning of the **English Civil War**. Parliament seized control of London and the King was forced to flee north. From that point on, the country's loyalties divided between those loyal to the king (**Royalists** or **"Cavaliers"**) and those loyal to the Parliament (**Parliamentarians** or **"Roundheads"**).

Charles' actions in marching into the House of Commons were thought to be so serious that no English monarch has set foot in the House of Commons since that day.

In this Civil War, like others, it is difficult to say clearly who supported each side. One village may have supported the King, while its neighbour was on Parliament's side. Indeed one of the saddest outcomes of the Civil War was that some families were divided, brother against brother and father against son. However, here are some groups who generally supported one side:

Supported Parliament	**Supported the King**
Puritans	Noblemen
Scots	Servants of noblemen
The Navy	Welsh
Farmers	
Townsfolk	
Merchants	

 TPD

ACTIVITY

Discuss the list of supporters of each side. Why do you think each group might have supported the side they did?

Oliver Cromwell, painted from life by Sir Peter Lely.

One of the key leaders of the Parliamentarians was an MP called **Oliver Cromwell**. He was born in 1599 in Huntingdon, and it is said that as a boy (in 1604) he fought the young Prince Charles I when Charles was staying at Cromwell's grandfather's home. The boys quarrelled over a toy and Cromwell is said to have made the Prince's nose bleed.

Cromwell was a strict Puritan, and became the greatest military commander on the Parliamentarian side.

Can you see the wart just above Cromwell's right eye? It is said that when this portrait was being painted the artist wanted to leave out the wart but Cromwell said, "Paint me warts and all!" We still use this phrase today.

Who was the English monarch when Cromwell was born?

UNIT 26: THE ENGLISH CIVIL WAR

CONFLICT

A Cavalier, who supported the King

A Roundhead, who supported Parliament

When the Civil War began in 1642 the King's supporters (the Cavaliers) and Parliament's supporters (the Roundheads) were evenly matched. At the beginning the King appeared to have an advantage, because the nobles who supported him were skilled horsemen, but this was more than wiped out by the formation of Parliament's **New Model Army**. This new army quickly proved itself to be a very professional and efficient force which would eventually guarantee Parliament's success in the Civil War.

Both armies were very similar: there were twelve regiments and each regiment had ten companies - a total of 1,200 men. Each company had its own flag. Companies had **musketeers** and **pikemen**, usually twice as many musketeers as pikemen. Much of the fighting was done by the musketeers, many of whom accidentally blew themselves up loading their muskets. Pikemen fought other pikemen and defended musketeers. The **cavalry** was organised in regiments and usually fought on the flanks of the army with the infantry in the centre. Many sieges also took place. For example, between April 1645 and August 1646, the New Model Army took part in eleven field battles and fifty sieges.

> **EFFICIENT: does its job well**
> **CAVALRY: soldiers mounted on horses**
> **FLANKS: the sides of something**

RESEARCH

Research each of these types of soldiers, making rough notes on what you find out: (a) musketeers (b) pikemen (c) cavalry. Think about things like these: How did they fight? What weapons did they use? What were the advantages and disadvantages of each?

Then, using your notes, write a paragraph on each type of soldier. When you have finished, add a few sentences saying which soldier you would prefer to have been and why. (Even if you would rather not fight at all, you have to choose one!)

TRY THIS

Imagine you are setting up a company of soldiers from your area. Design a flag for it, which shows some images that represent the area you come from. Display your flag designs in the classroom.

When the war started, the Cavaliers controlled northern England and Wales, but by 1645 they had lost control of almost all of England and half of Wales.

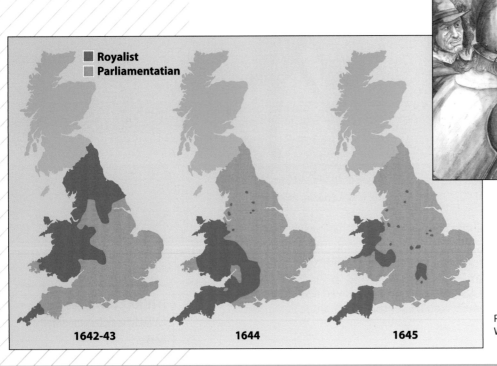

An artist's impression of a battle between Roundheads and Cavaliers.

Royalist
Parliamentatian

1642-43   1644   1645

Progress of the Civil War 1642-1645.

ACTIVITY

Talk about the picture of the battle scene. What does it tell you about how the battles were fought in the seventeenth century? How does this differ from the way wars are fought today? If a war has to be fought, which way is least harmful to non-fighting civilians?

CHARLES IS DEFEATED

In 1646 the King surrendered, and the New Model Army offered to let Charles remain King if he would agree to let everyone except Catholics worship as they pleased. The King was a proud man and as he did not want either Parliament or the army to dictate terms to him, he began plotting against Parliament. This resulted in the re-opening of the Civil War in 1648, but again Charles was decisively beaten. Naturally, the army generals were furious at the King's attempts to deceive them, and although many MPs in Parliament urged caution, the army was determined to execute Charles.

> **DICTATE TERMS: state what your opponent *must* agree to**
>
>

Why was Parliament determined to execute Charles in 1648 when they had offered to let him remain King in 1646?

This table shows the main events of the English Civil War:

1642	22 August	War declared.
	23 October	Battle of Edgehill – Royalist victory.
	13 November	King retreats to HQ in Oxford.
1643	January–May	Royalists do well in North, East, Midlands, Wales and Borders & West. Parliament does well in South and Central England.
	20 September	Inconclusive first battle of Newbury.
	25 September	20,000 Scottish troops come to help Parliament.
1644	19 January	Scottish army enters England.
	January–March	Royalist defeats in N Midlands and South.
	2 July	Cromwell wins at Marston Moor.
	27 October	Inconclusive second battle of Newbury.
1645	February	Unsuccessful peace negotiations.
	April	New Model Army created.
	14 June	Battle of Naseby.
	June–September	New Model Army has several victories.
1646	5 May	King surrenders to Scots and is taken to Newcastle.
	13 July	Peace terms presented to the King.
1647	March	Scottish army goes home.
	May	Short of money, Parliament pays off most of the New Model Army.
	June	Army refuses to retire until properly paid and a fair settlement reached with the King.
	1 August	Army puts forward its own peace terms.
	26 December	King persuades Scots to join his side and invade England.
1648	March–May	Royalists defeated by New Model Army in South East and Wales.
	2 August	Scots defeated at Preston.
	6 December	Army officers take over Parliament.
1649	20 January	This new Parliament puts the King on trial.
	27 January	Death sentence declared on the King.
	30 January	Charles I executed.
	February	House of Lords and Monarchy abolished.

Royalist in 1642
Parliamentatian
X Civil War battle

Marston Moor
Preston
Naseby
Edgehill
LONDON
Newbury

The main battles of the English Civil War

ACTIVITY

Form into pairs. Discuss the timeline of the Civil War. Decide which you think were the three most important events. Why do you think this?

CHARLES IS EXECUTED

Painting of Charles being executed.

In January 1649 the House of Commons set up a court to try the King. Part of the charge against him read:

> *Charles Stuart was made King ... yet out of a wicked design to erect and uphold an unlimited power to rule according to his will ... he has levied war against Parliament and the people that it represents.*

Charles was asked to reply to this charge but all he said was that he did not accept that the court had any right to put him on trial. However Charles was still declared guilty and sentenced to death on 27 January 1649. Only 59 of the 135 judges signed his death warrant.

His execution took place three days later. It is said that he asked for an extra vest so that he would not shiver with cold and make people think it was fear. On the scaffold he again claimed his innocence. His final words were *"I go from a corruptible to an uncorruptible crown, where no disturbance can be, no disturbance in the world".*

1. What did Charles I mean by these final words?
2. Do you think Oliver Cromwell would have agreed with him?
3. Why do you think only 59 of the judges signed the death warrant?
4. What percentage of the judges signed the death warrant? Give your answer to the nearest per cent.

ACTIVITY

You are one of the judges who has signed Charles I's death warrant. At home you write an entry on your blog describing the decision you had to take today and how you felt about being in the position of having to take this decision.

ACTIVITY

Using the material in Unit 25 and Unit 26, write an obituary of Charles I for (a) a Puritan newspaper, and (b) a Royalist newspaper.

ACTIVITY Class debate

"Charles I was executed because Parliament was greedy and just wanted more power for themselves."

Form two groups of about four. One group should argue **for** this motion and the other group must argue **against** it. The rest of the class will listen to the debate and at the end, vote on which side they feel has won the argument.

When writing anything, always remember to keep the target readership in mind.

It is thought that 17% of Parliamentarians and 12% of Royalists died in the nine major battles. At this time, the population of England was just over five million, of which 1.5 million were adult men. Disease also killed many. Plagues of typhoid and diarrhoea spread in many areas.

What is the population of England today, to the nearest million? How many times bigger is the population today than it was at the end of the English Civil War?

UNIT 27: OLIVER CROMWELL

LORD PROTECTOR

During the Civil War Oliver Cromwell emerged as the leading figure on the side of Parliament. He had started as an MP in 1640, but by 1646 he was a very successful general and the idol of the New Model Army. He also had great political gifts. Therefore, he was an ideal link between the army and Parliament. It was his position in the army, however, that enabled Cromwell to increase his own power, because it was the generals, and not Parliament, who were actually in charge of the country after the Civil War. By the early 1650s Cromwell was clearly the most powerful man in the country, and in 1653 he was given a new title, the **Lord Protector of the Commonwealth of England**, a position he held until his death in 1658.

Cromwell was a deeply religious man and tried to instil Puritan values on everyday life in England.

As a general in the army he believed that he was fighting God's battles. In politics he was convinced that every decision he made had to reflect God's will. There is no doubt that his sincere religious beliefs influenced his actions in Ireland in 1649–1650. This is what he said about his military victories:

> *"For these things that have lately come to pass have been the wonderful works of God; breaking the rod of the oppressor, as in the day of Midian..."*
>
> Cromwell in a letter to another general, Thomas Fairfax, June 1848

INSTIL: To introduce by constant efforts

OPPRESS: To be cruel and unjust to someone

In the Bible, "Midian" is a country that oppressed Israel, and God commanded Israel to destroy them. What do you think Cromwell meant by what he said to Thomas Fairfax? What does this tell us about Cromwell's motives?

Cromwell was so powerful that he could easily have made himself King. Why do you think he did not do so?

EFFECTS ON ENGLAND AND SCOTLAND

Cromwell is one of the most important figures in the history of the British Isles, and there is no doubt that he changed the course of English history. Parliament became more important, and the process by which power was transferred from the monarch to the people could not be stopped. One other consequence of Cromwell's rule was that future English governments were always careful to ensure that the army would never again become involved in politics.

England no longer had a king, and the House of Lords was abolished. In the Church, Bishops were abolished and each individual church was run by the minister and a committee elected by the congregation. Nearly all forms of entertainment (dancing, fairs, etc) were banned. Most people did not enjoy the strict conditions imposed by Puritan rule. Catholics were prosecuted if they tried to practise their religion.

Why do you think Cromwell made these changes?

Think of the consequences of banning nearly all forms of entertainment. Who would have been affected? Would people have lost their livelihood? Can you think of anyone who would have benefited?

The Scots were angered by Charles I's execution and they crowned his son, Prince Charles, as their King. He then led an army into England in an attempt to regain the throne but he was defeated by Cromwell.

Unlike many of the other great figures in history, Cromwell is remembered with little affection. The cruelty associated with his rule has influenced the way in which people think about him. Here are some things that historians have said about Cromwell:

> ... *a brave, bad man.*
>
> Earl of Clarendon, mid-17th century

> ... *a bulldozer who has wrecked civil life.*
>
> Andrew Maxwell, 1650

> ... *he inspired no fondness but profound mistrust even – perhaps especially – among men nearest him ... all complained at his slipperness.*
>
> Blair Worden, a 20th century historian

ACTIVITY

Look at the three quotations about Cromwell. Pick out words that are (a) favourable and (b) unfavourable to him.

What do you think Andrew Maxwell means by his comment?

DEATH OF CROMWELL

Cromwell died in 1658 at the age of 59 from an infection. He was buried in Westminster Abbey.

Why was it significant that Cromwell was buried in Westminster Abbey?

DISINTER: to dig up

After Cromwell's death his supporters quarrelled among themselves but were unable to govern the country firmly. By 1660 they decided to bring back the King. Charles II, the son of Charles I, agreed to rule on the conditions that his father had always rejected, and he became King in May 1660. The return of the monarchy is called **The Restoration**.

After the Restoration, Cromwell's body was disinterred and exposed to a mock execution on the gallows of Tyburn, before being thrown in a pit.

UNIT 28: CROMWELL IN IRELAND

THE ULSTER REBELLION

In Unit 25 you studied the rebellion in Ireland in 1641. Although many Irish Catholics were motivated by the loss of their land to English and Scottish planters, the conflict became part of the Civil War because the Irish Catholics sided with the King in his struggle against Parliament.

The stories of the massacre of Protestants were greatly exaggerated and by the time the Puritans in the House of Commons were told about these events, people in England believed that up to 300,000 Protestants had been slaughtered. Parliament was determined that this rebellion should be crushed and it was decided that the cost of the exercise would be paid for by confiscating more Irish land once the war was over.

Why do you think Irish Catholics sided with the English King in the Civil War?

The Civil War in England meant that only a small force could be sent to Ireland in **1642** and the result was military stalemate for the next seven years. This was to change in **1649** however when, following the King's execution, Parliament decided to send an army to Ireland to crush the enemies of the Commonwealth.

> **STALEMATE: when neither side can win a conflict**

ACTIVITY

Make two columns in your notebook. Title one column 'The Irish were…' and the other column 'The English were…'. The following statements are mixed up. Write them out in the correct column.

- sure that the Irish had behaved brutally in 1641
- Roman Catholic
- afraid the Irish could rebel at any time with foreign help
- angered that the English were taking their lands for plantations
- of the opinion that settlers in Ireland would be the best way of civilising Ireland
- aware that English did not understand Irish way of life
- angry that the English behaved brutally
- Protestant
- of the opinion that the Irish were backward savages

BREACH: to make a hole in something

CROMWELL ARRIVES

Cromwell himself took charge of the army (12,000 men), and it landed at **Ringsend** near Dublin in **August 1649**. One of the first actions of Cromwell's army was the capture of the town of Drogheda. It was occupied by a small force (a garrison) and after a very brief siege the town was stormed by Cromwell's troops in September 1649 after the walls had been breached by cannon fire. Most of the defending soldiers and many of the town's inhabitants were killed in this attack. This is how one eyewitness described the event:

> *When the city was captured by the heretics, the blood of the Catholics was mercilessly shed in the streets, in the dwelling houses and in the open fields. To none was mercy shown; not to women, nor to the aged, nor to the young. The majority of the citizens became the prey of the parliamentary troops.*
>
> A Jesuit Priest's eyewitness account of the attack on Drogheda.

Pick out the words and phrases in this account that suggest that the Jesuit priest was sympathetic to the townspeople and not to Cromwell. Is this a reliable account of the event? Explain your answer.

This is a more modern historian's view of the attack on Drogheda:

"Oliver Cromwell was sent to Ireland to deal with the Catholic rebellion. The methods he used to crush the rebels were harsh. When English soldiers captured the garrison of the town of Drogheda they ran wild, killing nearly 3000 people (including 200 women)".

From *The Irish Question* by Hamish Macdonald, 1985

Does Hamish Macdonald agree or disagree with the Jesuit priest?

News of this slaughter spread quickly with the result that neighbouring Catholic towns surrendered to avoid a repeat of the events in Drogheda. Cromwell's actions in Drogheda have been fiercely criticised by subsequent generations of Irishmen. He himself saw the massacre as fair punishment for the murder of Protestants in 1641. This is Cromwell's own report to Parliament in England about what happened at Drogheda in September 1649. Read this letter carefully and answer the questions that follow.

> *Sir,*
> *Your army came before the town of Drogheda on 3rd September. On Monday 9th the battering guns [cannon] began to play [fire at the town]. I sent ... a summons to deliver the town [surrender]. Receiving no satisfactory answer, the guns fired two or three hundred shot, beat down the corner tower, and opened up two reasonable breaches in the east and south wall.*

Upon Tuesday the 10th, about five o'clock in the evening, we began the storm [attacked the town] and after some hot fighting we entered, about seven or eight hundred men, the enemy disputing it very stiffly with us. Several of the enemy retreated to the Mill Mount, a place very strong and difficult to attack. ... Our men getting up to them were ordered by me to put all to the sword. And indeed, being in the heat of the action, I forbade them to spare any people who carried weapons in the town and I think that night they put to the sword 2,000 men. Many of their officers and soldiers fled over the bridge into the other part of the town, where about 100 of them [went into] St Peter's church steeple. These being summoned to yield to mercy, refused, whereupon I ordered the steeple of St Peter's Church to be fired [set on fire]....

The next day the other two towers were [asked to surrender], in one of which was about six or seven score soldiers. But they refused to yield. We knew that hunger must force them and set good guards to stop them running away. When they surrendered, their officers were knocked on the head [killed] and every tenth man of the soldiers killed. The rest were captured.

The last Lord's Day before the storm, they had a Mass in St Peter's Church. About one thousand Catholics were put to the sword, fleeing there for safety. I believe all the friars [Catholic preachers] were knocked on the head except two. One the soldiers captured and made an end of [killed]. The other was captured in the round tower. He confessed he was a friar, but that did not save him.

I believe that this is a righteous judgement of God upon these barbarous wretches, who have dipped their hands in so much innocent blood murdered many innocent people. And it will help to prevent more bloodshed in the future. It was God who gave your men courage. It is good that God has all the glory. I do not think we lost 100 men, though many be wounded.

Your most obedient servant,
Oliver Cromwell.

1. If there are any words you didn't understand, look them up.
2. Choose words from the following list to describe the tone of Cromwell's letter. Humble, jubilant, sorry, remorseful, happy, confident, frightened, smug, factual, unbiased, aggressive, proud.
3. What sentence shows that Cromwell wants his actions to frighten other towns in Ireland?
4. How does Cromwell justify his actions?
5. From reading this letter, would you hold Cromwell personally responsible for all the deaths? Explain your opinion.

Antonia Fraser, in her modern biography of Cromwell, said this:

The conclusion cannot be escaped that Cromwell lost his self-control at Drogheda, literally saw red – the red of his comrades' blood – after the failure of the first assaults, and was seized with one of his sudden brief and cataclysmic rages. There were good military reasons for behaving as he did, but they were not the motives that drove him at the time, during the day and night of uncalculated butchery. The slaughter itself stood quite outside his normal record of careful mercy as a soldier.

Cromwell, our Chief of Men, Antonia Fraser, Phoenix, 2002

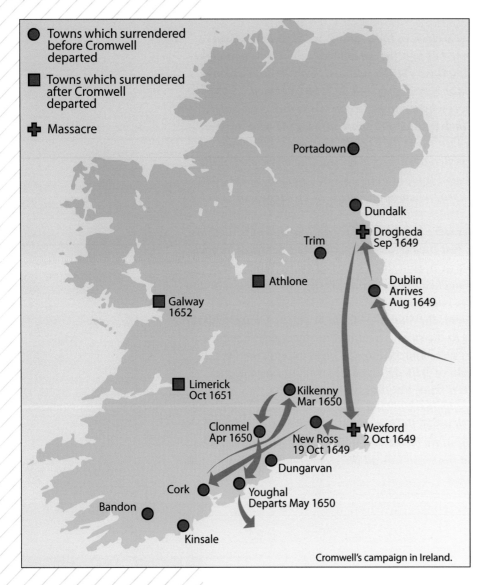

Legend:
- Towns which surrendered before Cromwell departed
- Towns which surrendered after Cromwell departed
- Massacre

Portadown

Dundalk

Drogheda Sep 1649

Trim

Athlone

Dublin Arrives Aug 1649

Galway 1652

Limerick Oct 1651

Kilkenny Mar 1650

Clonmel Apr 1650

New Ross 19 Oct 1649

Wexford 2 Oct 1649

Dungarvan

Cork

Youghal Departs May 1650

Bandon

Kinsale

Cromwell's campaign in Ireland.

After Drogheda, Cromwell marched his troops south, and a similar attack took place on Wexford and once again many of the Catholic residents were massacred. For Cromwell this had the desired effect as the neighbouring towns of New Ross, Cork, Bandon, Kinsale and Youghal quickly surrendered, once news of the events in Wexford reached them. Other towns surrendered in the spring of 1650 and although some fighting continued for a further two years, Cromwell was able to leave Ireland in 1650 in the knowledge that he had obtained a crushing victory over the Catholic rebels.

ACTIVITY

Create a timeline of Oliver Cromwell's campaign in Ireland.

ACTIVITY

Write a Wikipedia article under the title "Cromwell's Attack on Drogheda".

Write one or two sentences at the start to summarise the significance of the event. Then describe in your own words what happened. Remember to **cite** your sources, which can be from this Unit, or from anything else you have studied.

UNIT 29: THE CROMWELLIAN SETTLEMENT

TO HELL OR CONNACHT

As well as taking revenge against the Irish Catholics for the rebellion they began in 1641, Cromwell knew he had an economic reason for having to conquer Ireland. This bar sets out the economic reasoning:

| The Civil War had involved many soldiers | Officers in the New Model Army had not been paid | The government in London had taken out lots of loans | The government had run out of money | Cromwell decided to pay the soldiers who had fought the Irish campaign with grants of land | The land was seized from the Catholic rebels after their defeat. |

In fact, Cromwell's control of Ireland was guaranteed when nearly 35,000 of the defeated Catholic soldiers decided to leave Ireland to join the armies of Catholic France and Spain. The English government hoped that its control over Ireland could be extended by a new scheme of plantation, similar to the Ulster Plantation. However the government was unable to attract enough Protestant settlers to Ireland, and the attempted plantation was a failure.

For what reasons might Protestants not want to settle in Ireland?

In 1652 the **Cromwellian Settlement** was passed by Parliament. It transferred all wealth and power to Protestants. Most Catholic landowners had to give up their land to new Protestant landowners. This meant that ordinary Catholics were allowed to stay in their homes, but their rents were paid to the new landowners. A number of Catholic landowners were allowed to keep some property, but they still had to leave their traditional lands and instead take much smaller and poorer holdings in the west. County Clare and most of the counties in Connacht were reserved for these Catholic landowners and their families. The west had the poorest farming land in Ireland, and the Catholics who were sent there were not allowed to live in towns or within three miles of the coast, as all coastal land was given to Cromwellian soldiers.

It was said that Cromwell gave the choice to Irish Catholic landowners in the words: they could go "to Hell or Connacht".

ACTIVITY

It is 1652. You are fourteen years old and you have lived in county Waterford all your life. Your father has just told you and the rest of your family that you will have to leave your home and travel to Connacht to live. Write a diary entry in which you describe how this news has affected the different members of your family as well as yourself. Include thoughts on how you will prepare for the journey and how will you travel. Are you excited, depressed, afraid? What about your friends?

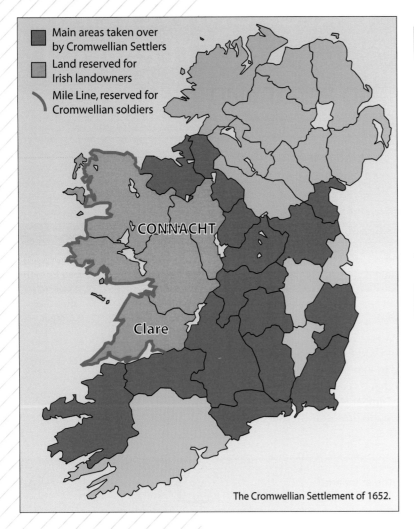

Legend:
- Main areas taken over by Cromwellian Settlers
- Land reserved for Irish landowners
- Mile Line, reserved for Cromwellian soldiers

CONNACHT

Clare

The Cromwellian Settlement of 1652.

1. The Irish province of Connacht contains five counties. Find out their names.

2. According to the map, three areas of Ireland were not part of the Cromwellian Settlement. Suggest why this might be the case.

3. Suggest what the consequences of the Cromwellian Settlement were in Connacht.

Find out why the west of Ireland has the poorest farming land in Ireland. What is different there compared to eastern parts of Ireland? Suggest why the coast was reserved for Cromwellian soldiers. Write about 150 words explaining your findings.

The amount of land owned by Catholics in Ireland declined from about 60% to less than 10% after the Cromwellian Settlement.

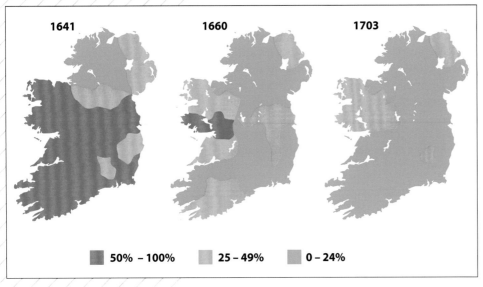

1641   1660   1703

- 50% – 100%
- 25 – 49%
- 0 – 24%

Map showing lands owned by Catholics in 1641, 1660 and 1703.

1. In which areas did Catholics continue to hold at least 25% of the land between 1641 and 1703?

2. Suggest why they lost land in other areas.

3. Did Catholics lose more land in the period 1641–1660 or in the period 1660–1703? Explain your conclusion.

RELIGIOUS PERSECUTION

Not surprisingly, Cromwell's government in England, which was dominated by Puritans, did all it could to make life very difficult for Catholics. Many were executed, while others were imprisoned or forced to leave the country. Indeed most of the Catholic clergy, numbering about l,000 priests, were forced out of Ireland in the 1650s. This is what Cromwell wrote about the policy towards Catholics:

> *I meddle not with any man's conscience, but if by liberty of conscience you mean a liberty to exercise the Mass, I judge it best to use plain dealing, and let you know, where the Parliament of England have power, that will not be allowed.*

Oliver Cromwell, 1650

1. What do each of these phrases mean?
    (a) "I meddle not with any man's conscience"
    (b) "a liberty to exercise the Mass"
    (c) "I judge it best to use plain dealing"
2. What is Cromwell's attitude towards people's right to practice their own religion, according to this quote?

When Charles II became King in 1660, he made very few changes to the Cromwellian land settlement, but he did relax the persecution against the Catholic Church in Ireland.

ACTIVITY

In groups draw up a list of points, based on the material in Unit 28 and Unit 29:
    (a) **for** Oliver Cromwell
    (b) **against** Oliver Cromwell

Then imagine you are an Irish Catholic. Using the evidence you have compiled, write a letter to the *Drogheda Times* giving your opinion of Oliver Cromwell's time in Ireland.

ACTIVITY

Class Debate

"Cromwell was a cruel dictator who oppressed the people".

Form into two groups. One of the groups must give reasons to support this statement. The other group must argue that the statement is unfair, and find positive things about Cromwell. At the end of the debate, vote on which side made the better argument.

REVIEW THIS SECTION

Review this section

How much did you know about the events in this section before you started it?

Have you changed your opinion about anything?

Was there any topic that provoked a lot of discussion in class? If so, why?

If you could go back in time and witness one of the events you have learnt about, which one would it be?

MI

TPD

BC

WO

ACTIVITY

Put together a timeline of all the events you learnt about between Unit 23 and Unit 29. You could split the timeline into sections and different groups could be responsible for compiling and illustrating different bits of it.

Put your timeline up on the classroom wall and when you are finished, talk about each entry on it.

If there is anything you didn't understand, now is your chance to ask!

Word Check

Check out these words to make sure you can spell them.

campaign	Monteagle	Anglican
Restoration	Parliamentarian	settlement
Cromwell	government	suspicious
Puritans	guarantee	interview
Cavaliers	conscience	illegal
cellar	corruptible	authorised
rebellion	religious	

If you're not sure if you can spell any of them, check them out a few more times.

Class Quiz!

Divide into two teams and decide on a prize for the winning team. If you get a question right, your team gets a point, BUT if you get a question wrong, you lose a point! So think carefully before you answer.

1. "The Roundheads supported the King." Is this True or false?

2. What year was the King James Bible first issued?

3. Who was given the choice, "To Hell or Connacht"?

4. Who was James I and VI's mother?

5. What is "The Divine Right of Kings"?

6. Who was given the title "Lord Protector of the Commonwealth of England"?

7. What was the name of the ship in which the Pilgrim Fathers sailed to America?

8. The Gunpowder Plot was a plot to blow up which building?

9. Where did Cromwell and his army land in Ireland in 1649?

10. What did James I and VI call 'a filthie noveltie'?

11. What was the purpose of the Monteagle Letter?

12. In what year was Charles I executed?

13. Who do we regard as the main plotter in the Gunpowder Plot?

14. What was the first town attacked by Cromwell when he landed in Ireland?

15. Name two of the three main religious groups in England in the time of James I.

16. Complete this sentence: "Cromwell decided to pay the _____ in the Irish campaign with grants of _____."

17. Did Puritans dress elaborately or simply?

18. Under the Cromwellian Settlement, who took land round the coast of Connacht?

19. How many judges signed Charles I's death warrant?

20. What and when was The Restoration?

Before you start

On a blank map of Ireland, mark the following:

Belfast, the River Boyne, Derry/Londonderry, Limavady, Aughrim, Enniskillen, Dublin, Limerick, the Province of Connacht, Drogheda, New Ross, Cork, Bandon, Kinsale, Youghal, Wexford, Carrickfergus, Dundalk, Athlone, Antrim, Omagh, Strabane.

Swap maps with a partner and check the accuracy of your partner's map.

Keep your map so that you can refer to it when you come to events on Ireland in this Section.

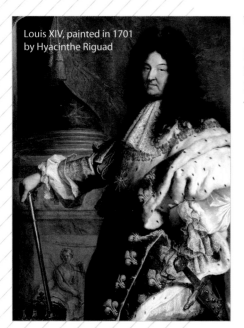

Louis XIV, painted in 1701 by Hyacinthe Riguad

WAR IN EUROPE

In 1688 war broke out in Europe between the French King, **Louis XIV**, and a league of European states, known as the **Grand Alliance** who wanted to stop Louis' attempts to expand his kingdom. This war lasted until 1697.

The Grand Alliance was led by **William of Orange** and included:

- the Spanish King whose Empire included the Spanish Netherlands (Holland);
- the Holy Roman Emperor who ruled a collection of German states; and
- the rulers of Prussia and Bavaria.

Europe in 1688
- Members of Grand Alliance 1689
- France and her Allies
- Ottoman Empire
- - - Boundary of Holy Roman Empire

Sweden
Denmark
Prussia
Ireland
Britain Holland
Poland
Holy Roman Empire
Bavaria
Hungary
France
Ottoman Empire
Portugal
Spain
Naples
Ottoman Empire

MI

ACTIVITY

Study the map and compare it to a map of Europe today.

What countries still exist much as they did in 1688?

Make a list of the countries that have disappeared.

Make a list of ten countries that exist in Europe now but did not exist in 1688.

Some kings and rulers who were not members of the Grand Alliance still wanted Louis defeated so that Europe could be at peace. **James II** of England did not join the Alliance in 1688 because he felt that England was in no danger at that time. Besides, he wanted to remain on good terms with both the Dutch and the French.

James had become King of England in 1685 and, even though he was a Catholic, no one really objected to him. However, there was one small rebellion led by the Duke of Monmouth. After this, James kept a large army and also promoted many Catholics to officer status. He tried to introduce forms of religious tolerance for non-Anglicans (people who were not members of the Church of England).

Parliament became increasingly suspicious of him and feared that he was trying to make England a Catholic country. There was also concern that he might persecute Protestants as Louis XIV was doing in France. James had only two daughters and no sons at this time, so the heir to the throne was his elder daughter, Mary, who had married William of Orange.

Why do we say Mary was James' 'elder' daughter and not his 'eldest' daughter?

THE GLORIOUS REVOLUTION

In June 1688, however, James' second wife **Mary of Modena** had a son. This changed things dramatically. This boy, who was to be brought up Catholic, would now succeed his father, displacing his two older Protestant sisters, Mary and Anne. To prevent a Catholic becoming king, the English Parliament invited William of Orange, James' daughter Mary's husband, to take the English throne.

Why did James' son become the heir to the throne even though he had two half-sisters who were born before him?

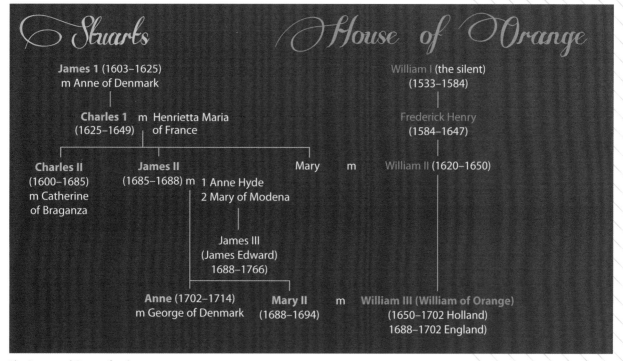

The Stuart and Orange family trees.

ACTIVITY

Hot seat!

Elect one person to be William of Orange and another to be James II. They must sit at the front of the class and debate with one another about who should be heir to the throne – William or James' son. As they debate, anyone in the class can put their hand up to ask a question of either of them. At the end, have a vote on who seems to you to have the stronger claim.

Mary II, wife of William of Orange and daughter of James II.

William landed on the south coast of England in November 1688 and moved to London. Because James II didn't have widespread support, he fled to France with his wife and son. William and Mary were made joint monarchs in February 1689 as William III and Mary II. This is known as the **Glorious Revolution**. William had been eager to come to England, because he hoped to add England's forces to the Grand Alliance to help the struggle against Louis XIV. However, he soon found that his attention was diverted by events in Ireland.

ACTIVITY

To understand the Glorious Revolution it is important to understand all the family relationships at the time. Study the family tree on the previous page. Form into groups, get a pad of Post-it notes, choose a 'runner', and play this game.

All the runners must stand at the back of the room. Your teacher will call out the questions below. If you know the answer, write it **clearly** on a Post-it note and take it to the runner for your group. The runner must stick it on the wall at the front of the classroom as fast as he or she can. The first runner to get there gets a point for the group – but only if the answer is right!

1. Who was Charles I's father?
2. Who was Charles II's brother, who became king after him?
3. Who was James II's second wife?
4. Who was William of Orange's father-in-law?
5. Which King married Mary of Modena?
6. What was their son called?
7. Who was Charles II's mother?
8. What relation to Anne Hyde was Mary II?
9. Did Mary II marry her (a) uncle (b) cousin or (c) brother-in-law?
10. Was Charles II of the House of Stuart or the House of Orange?

ACTIVITY

Write a letter from Mary to her sister Anne, in November 1688, explaining her position as daughter of the deposed King and the wife of the new one.

DEPOSED: removed from a position of power

DERRY AND ENNISKILLEN

The result of the Cromwellian Settlement of 1652 had been to divide Irish society into **landowners** on one side and a great number of small tenant-farmers, called **cottiers**, on the other.

During James' reign things had got better for Catholics, just as had happened in England. Now that James II was king, many former landowners also hoped that he would give them back their estates.

In 1687 James made his friend, **Richard Talbot, Earl of Tyrconnell** the Lord Lieutenant – the King's representative in Ireland. Talbot strengthened the Irish army in case it was needed to support James, and appointed Catholics to key leadership roles in the army and government. Talbot was a Catholic and was quickly nicknamed **'Lying Dick'** by Protestants.

Tyrconnell was anxious that all the major towns in Ireland should be occupied by armies loyal to King James. So in 1688 Tyrconnell sent troops to Derry and Enniskillen, because they were the only two places which did not fully support James. However the garrisons in Derry and Enniskillen refused to let them in, in direct defiance of the Lord Lieutenant. In Derry, thirteen apprentice boys seized the keys of the city gates and closed them. This is how the event was described by two different people:

James II, painted by Sir Peter Lely

> *... we had been alarmed by reports that the Roman Catholics intended to rise in arms against us and to act over the tragedy of 1641 ... At last a regiment of them ... actually arrived at Newtownlimavady, on their march to Derry ... These set us immediately to consider what was to be done; but we could not determine among ourselves what was best. While we were in this confused hesitation, on the 7 December 1688, a few resolute apprentice boys determined for us. These ran to the Gates and shut them, drew up the bridge, and seized the magazine. This, like magic, roused an unanimous spirit of defence and now with one voice we determined to maintain the city at all hazards, and each sex and age joined in the important cause.*
>
> Thomas Ash, a Protestant from Londonderry

DEFIANCE: not obeying direct instructions

MAGAZINE: a place where weapons are kept

ACTIVITY

Thomas Ash writes a blog on events he is witnessing in Derry in 1688. Compose his blog entries for the 5th, 6th and 7th of December. Remember he is an eyewitness and his feelings are very fresh.

 COM

 ICT

BC

BURGESSES: people who lived in a town

> The first of Ireland's Protestants who appeared [in support of] the Prince of Orange were the inhabitants of Londonderry.
> The burgesses hearing ... that the king was abandoned by his army and by the people of England, did resolutely, about the beginning of December 1688, shut up their gates against the said regiment ... About the same time the viceroy sent two companies to be quartered at Enniskillen, a small inland town in the same province. This also refused entrance to the king's garrison.
>
> Nicholas Plunkett, a Jacobite supporter of Tyrconnell

Artist's impression of the apprentice boys closing the gates of Derry as Tyrconnell's troops approach.

ACTIVITY

Compare the two accounts of the closing of the gates of Derry, by Thomas Ash and by Nicholas Plunkett. In what ways are the two accounts different. Suggest a reason for the differences. Do these differences make the sources unreliable? Explain your answer.

Which account seems more biased? Would you say that one of them is more neutral?

ACTIVITY

You are a resident of Derry, and have just witnessed the Apprentice Boys closing the gates of the city. You are feeling both nervous and excited. Write two letters to a relative in another part of Ulster. The first one is from a Catholic resident of Derry and the other from a Protestant resident. Explain what has happened, why it has happened and what you hope will happen next. Remember you live in 1688, not today!

ACTIVITY Class debate

Organise a debate on the following motion:

"This House believes it is important to remember past events for hundreds of years."

Remember that to put a case for or against this motion, you must give reasons why it is or why it is not important and use examples.

At the end, take a vote on the motion.

Did anyone change his or her mind as a result of the debate? If so, why?

WAR LOOMS

Protestants in Ireland declared their support for William and Mary and prepared to fight for them. Those who supported William are usually call **Williamites**, while James' supporters are known as **Jacobites**. A leading Ulster Jacobite was the **Earl of Antrim**. This is what Tyrconnell told the Earl of Antrim that he would do if the people of Londonderry did not let his army in:

> *Finding the people of Londonderry continue obstinate to their rebellion, and that there appears no likelihood of reducing them by fair means. I desire your lordship to give orders presently, to all the companies of your regiment, to be in readiness to march at an hours warning, it being my resolution in case I doe not hear, by fridays post, that the City of Derry has submitted, to order them, with several other regiments of horse, foot and dragoons, to march against it, and will soon follow them myself.*

Letter from the Earl of Tyrconnell to the Earl of Antrim, 1688

ACTIVITY

Pick out words and phrases in the letter from Tyrconnell that show:

(a) that he wants the problem at Londonderry to be solved urgently, and

(b) that he does not think that the residents will give up without a fight.

ACTIVITY

Extended writing

You have been asked to contribute to a web site dealing with events in Ireland in the late seventeenth century. Your task is to compile a short section explaining why Protestants tended to support William of Orange and Catholics tended to support James.

Word-process your piece. When you are satisfied that it is as good as you can make it, e-mail it as an attachment to another person in the class. The person who receives it should send back an acknowledgement of receipt.

CONDITIONS IN THE CITY

In the last Unit we read how the apprentice boys of Derry had shut the gates against the advancing Jacobite army in December 1688. To some people in the City of Derry this was seen as treason against their lawful King, James. For others, this action was vital for their security.

James had lost his throne in England in November 1688 and fled to France. From there, he came to Ireland in **March 1689**, determined to crush all remaining opposition. One of his first actions was to demand the surrender of Derry, the Williamite stronghold, which was then under the command of **Robert Lundy**. This marked the beginning of the siege, which would last 105 days. Governor Lundy and the city council considered surrendering. The residents of Derry were so angry at him for this that he had to flee from the town. The **Rev George Walker** became the new Governor of the city. On **4 June 1689** a boom was placed across the River Foyle leaving those defending the city cut off and running very short of supplies.

> **VITAL: absolutely necessary**

> **BOOM: floating barrier**

TPD

Q Why do you think blocking the River Foyle was important for cutting off supply to the city?

Date	Big	Small
April 24 – 27	0	17
April 27 – 6 May	0	6
June 2 – 21 July	261	326
July 22	0	42
July 23	0	20

Cannon shot or mortar bombs fired at the City of Derry in 1689

MA **Q** Study the table on the left. How many **small** shots/mortars were fired at the City of Derry in total, according to the table?

Many of the cannon used by the defenders can still be seen on the walls today.

Conditions in the city deteriorated. The defenders were short of ammunition, food and supplies. They also suffered from many diseases. Here are some accounts of what life was like in the city:

> **DETERIORATED: got worse**

> *Our drink was nothing but water, which we paid very dear for, and could not get without danger.*
>
> George Walker, Governor of Derry

> *Everyday some ... deserted the garrison, so that the enemy received constant intelligence of our proceedings. This gave some trouble and made us remove our ammunition very often ... Our iron-ball is now all spent, and instead of them we make balls of brick, cast over with lead, to the weight and size of our iron-ball.*
>
> George Walker, Governor of Derry

... the cold which the men – specially the women and children – contracted, hereby, added to their want of rest and food, occasioned diseases in the garrison, as fevers, flux, etc of which great numbers died.

John Mackenzie, Protestant chaplain to Walker's regiment

 Look at the price list on the right. How much would it cost in **total** to buy a quarter of a dog, a cat and a mouse? Write your answer in shillings and pence.

The people of Derry could have ended the siege by surrendering to the Jacobite forces. Why, when their conditions were so bad, did they choose not to surrender?

  ## ACTIVITY

Form groups. You are reporters for a 1689 version of the TV news. Construct a report from the City of Derry, describing living conditions in the city and the difficulties caused by the besieging Jacobite forces. If you have time, you could make a video of your report and let the rest of the class watch it.

Food was so scarce that the prices soared. Here are the prices of some items of food in the city during the siege:

A pound of horse	1s 8d
A quarter of a dog	5s 6d
A dog's head	2s 6d
A cat	4s 6d
A pound of tallow	4s 0d
A pound of salted Hides	1s 0d
A quarter of horse blood	1s 0d
A rat	1s 0d
A mouse	0s 6d
A horse pudding	0s 6d
A handful of chick weed	0s 1d
A quart of meal when found	1s 0d

Note: 1s means one shilling and 1d means one penny. There were 12 pennies in a shilling.

THE SIEGE ENDS

A relief force arrived in Lough Foyle on 13 June but did not try to break through the boom. The ship's captain claimed that when he had not heard from the city's defenders, he assumed they did not need his help. Eventually on **28 July** the ship's captain, Major-General Kirke, was ordered by the government in London to break the boom. The ship, called *The Mountjoy*, broke the boom, ending the siege. The soldiers who had followed James left as quickly as possible. Both armies suffered heavy casualties.

While the siege was taking place in Derry, the garrison at **Enniskillen** intercepted the Jacobites at Newtownbutler and forced them to divide their forces, keeping half the Jacobite army from going to Derry. In August an English general, **Frederick Schomberg**, landed at Carrickfergus, captured it after a brief siege, and soon all of Ulster was in Williamite hands.

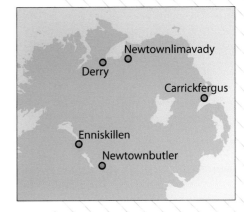

Places involved in the conflict in 1689.

ACTIVITY
Here are three facts:
- In 1826 a memorial to George Walker was erected on Derry's City Walls.
- This memorial was destroyed by the IRA in 1973.
- Every December an effigy of Robert Lundy is burned by the *Apprentice Boys*.

What is the significance of each of these three facts? What does each one tell us about how different people view the Siege of Derry? Why is there so much disagreement?

 EFFIGY: an object made to look like a person

UNIT 33: THE WAR OF THE THREE KINGS

William III

THE TWO ARMIES

By the time James had arrived in Ireland from France in March 1689, many groups of Protestants throughout Ulster were fighting back. When they were unsuccessful, many fled to England or Scotland, while some took refuge in fortified towns such as Derry, as you learnt in the the previous Unit.

The quarrel that was emerging between William and James was part of the on-going war in Europe between the French King, Louis XIV, and the Grand Alliance, led by William (see Unit 30). In fact, the Pope was against the French King and had special prayers of thanksgiving said in Rome when news reached him that William had defeated James, because James was supported by the French.

Because of Louis XIV's involvement, the **Williamite Wars** are sometimes known in Ireland as the **War of the Three Kings**. It lasted from 1688 to 1691. During this time there were several major battles.

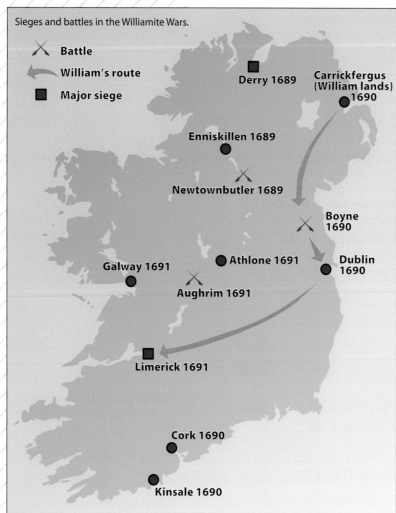

Sieges and battles in the Williamite Wars.

- ✕ **Battle**
- ⬅ **William's route**
- ■ **Major siege**

Derry 1689

Carrickfergus (William lands) 1690

Enniskillen 1689

Newtownbutler 1689

Boyne 1690

Galway 1691

Athlone 1691

Dublin 1690

Aughrim 1691

Limerick 1691

Cork 1690

Kinsale 1690

On James II's side, the main army leaders were his brother-in-law, the Earl of Tyrconnell and **Patrick Sarsfield** (above) who was the defender of Limerick. The Jacobite forces in Ireland consisted of 25,000 men of whom 6,000 were French, who had been in battle before. The rest were inexperienced. He had no cannon and just twelve French field pieces. The soldiers had scythes or sharpened sticks.

> **ARTILLERY :** large guns that fire a projectile, eg cannon
>
> **FIELD PIECE:** small artillery that can be moved easily

General Godert de Ginkel, a Williamite commander

The Williamite forces were larger in number and better equipped. William had 36,000 men including Blue Dutch Guards, Danes, German Branden-burgers and French Protestants. These soldiers were well-trained mercenaries. They had good artillery with 50 to 60 large cannon and several mortars. They also had up-to-date flintlock muskets and bayonets. Two major army leaders were **Godert de Ginkel**, a Dutchman who became First Earl of Athlone and fought at the Battle of Aughrim; and the **Duke of Schomberg** who was killed at the Boyne.

MERCENARY: a soldier who hires himself out for money

MORTAR: a type of artillery; can fire accurately at short distances

Godert de Ginkel was Dutch, yet became a commander of the Williamite army in Ireland. Why do you think a Dutch man ended up in Ireland?

Look at the drawing of the seventeenth century siege guns.

Why was it necessary to cool the gun after firing? What would have happened if they re-loaded it without cooling it?

UNIFORMS

The two armies did not have a set uniform, so there was a great deal of confusion in identifying who was who. For example, here are some of the colours worn by each army:

- Jacobites – white; or yellow; or blue; or red with orange lining; or red with white lining; or white with red lining.

- Williamites – blue; or white; or buff coats with coloured sashes; or red with yellow facings; or blue with yellow facings; or green with white facings.

The problem was so bad that the commanders had to instruct their soldiers to wear objects to identify who was who:

> *Orders were given out that ... every man [should wear] a green Bough or Sprig in his Hat to distinguish him from the Enemy (who wore pieces of paper in their Hats).*
>
> George Story, author of a book about the wars in Ireland, published in 1691

Seventeenth century siege guns: firing (top), cooling the barrel (middle), cooling the breech with sheepskins soaked in water (bottom).

RESEARCH

Choose four sports teams, and find out what colours they wear when they are playing. Draw or paint the sports strip for each one.

Why do sports teams have colours? What would happen if everyone in a match wore the same colours?

Why would it be a problem for an army not to have a set uniform? The commanders in 1689 didn't have time to make and give out uniforms, so they solved the problem by putting a piece of paper or a green sprig in their hats. Do you think this was a good solution? Why or why not?

THE BATTLE OF THE BOYNE

At the beginning of March 1690 four thousand Danes arrived in Belfast to help William. Within a week, more reinforcements had arrived from England. Many of the Danes were keen to end the war in Ireland and bring William back to take charge once again of the Grand Alliance in the European conflict.

At the same time Louis XIV agreed to send James some battle-hardened French soldiers. Louis wanted the war to continue in Ireland so that William would be kept out of the European conflict.

In June 1690 William arrived at **Carrickfergus** and marched on Dundalk. James moved north from Dublin to meet him. On **1 July 1690** the two armies met at the **River Boyne** in County Meath.

 The spot where the Danish forces arrived is now part of Newtownabbey, and there is a park there, called Gideon's Green. A memorial stone marks the site.

RESEARCH

The calendar used in Britain and Ireland was later adjusted by 11 days, so today the date of the battle is remembered as **12 July 1690**.

In 1752 Britain changed from the Julian calendar to the Gregorian calendar, which was the reason for adjusting the date. Find out:

    (a) what these two calendars were
    (b) why they were different
    (c) why the date had to be changed by 11 days
    (d) what objections people had to the change.

Word-process your findings and present them in a short report.

The weather was good on the day William and James met:

> *The day was very clear, as if the Sun itself had a mind to see what would happen.*
>
> George Story, a chaplain in Schomberg's army

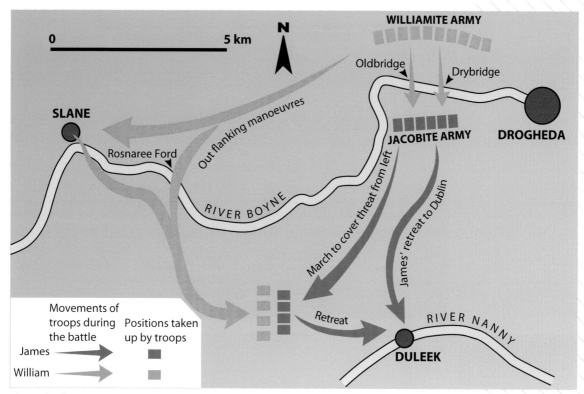

The Battle of the Boyne

James believed that William's main attack would come from Rosnaree so he moved more than half of his army in that direction. However, at that point the ground was marshy and no fighting was to take place there.

Instead the Williamite army crossed between Oldbridge and Drybridge. The Duke of Schomberg and the Rev George Walker were killed there.

Although the Jacobites were heavily outnumbered, the battle lasted for two hours. William's army crossed the river first and the Jacobite cavalry fought well. When James saw that the battle was lost, he fled with his bodyguard to Dublin, before setting sail for France. The Jacobite losses numbered about 1,300, while the Williamites lost about 400.

Because William was part of the European Grand Alliance, there was rejoicing throughout Europe that he had defeated an ally of Louis XIV.

One modern comedian joked that, after he had lost at the Boyne, James was told, "Don't worry about it; in two weeks nobody will remember a thing about it!"

ACTIVITY

In groups, make a list of reasons for either:

Why William won at the Boyne,

OR

Why James lost at the Boyne.

List as many reasons as you can, and then pick out what you think is the most important reason. Mark this as number one and rank all the rest in order of importance.

Choose a 'reporter' in each group, who will report back to the class on their group's conclusions.

MI

TPD

WO

A modern Orange Banner showing King William crossing the Boyne.

ACTIVITY

Use the library or the Internet to find pictures of William and James at the Boyne. Suggest why many differences appear in these pictures.

Why do you think some people commemorate the Battle of the Boyne today?

Why would some people not wish to commemorate the Battle today?

Find out if William's horse was really white.

ACTIVITY

Read this extract from a modern analysis of the forces of William and James in 1690.

"As for the Boyne being a Catholic v Protestant affair, this aspect of it is greatly exaggerated. William's army of 36,000 was a multi national force made up of Germans, Danes, Dutch, Finns, French, Swiss, Ulstermen and Scots. Surprisingly few English troops were involved as William didn't trust them to fight their former king. Many of William's men were Catholics and his Dutch Blue Guards regiment carried the Papal Banner at The Boyne."

From: iancolquhoun.org.uk/myths-about-the-boyne, accessed 25 July 2011

Take each sentence in this comment one at a time. Write out the sentence and then write your own comments beneath it. For example, say whether the sentence contains anything that surprises you; whether you believe it; the reason why the writer says what he says. Add any other observations you would like to make.

Do this for each of the four sentences.

When you have finished, discuss your findings in class.

UNIT 34: LIMERICK AND AUGHRIM

THE SIEGE OF LIMERICK

After the Battle of the Boyne, Tyrconnell was prepared to negotiate with William. However, some other Jacobites such as Sarsfield refused to do so. They hoped for better peace terms from William if they could hold out for longer. The rest of the Irish army was concentrated in **Limerick** and **Athlone**. Early in August 1690 William laid siege to Limerick. Patrick Sarsfield led the defenders there. He managed to intercept and destroy a great quantity of William's guns at Ballineedy.

This was a major blow for William, and although he was still able to launch an attack on Limerick, the Jacobites were able to hold out. Here are two accounts of the attack:

> *William, having made a larger breach in the wall, gave a general assault which lasted for three hours; and though his men mounted the breach, and some even entered the town, they were gallantly repulsed and forced to retire with considerable loss.*

Charles O'Kelly (1621–95), a Irish soldier and author, writing about the siege at Limerick

> *The Irish ventured upon the breach again, and from the walls and every place so pestered us upon the counterscarp, that after nigh three hours resisting bullets, stones, broken bottles ... and whatever way could be thought on to destroy us, our ammunition being spent, it was judged safest to return to our trenches.*

George Story (1664–1721), a Protestant chaplain in the Williamite army

REPULSED: driven back

COUNTERSCARP: the ditch on the inside of a defensive wall

ACTIVITY

Discuss these two accounts of the battle. Pick out words and phrases that indicate whether each one is sympathetic to the Williamites or the Jacobites. What impression does each one give of the Irish forces? According to each source, what was the reason for the Williamites retreating from the battle? Are the two accounts different? If so, why do you think this is?

As autumn and the heavy rains set in, William finally gave up and left Ireland. He never returned. He left General Ginkel in charge. Ginkel offered peace to Sarsfield and the Jacobites. They rejected this, however, and decided to fight on. Ginkel then prepared for a final assault. By this time, the Jacobites had another leader, a French General called **Marquis de St Ruth**.

Why do you think William left Ireland? What does this tell us about his opinion of the war in Ireland by this point?

THE BATTLE OF AUGHRIM

By the summer of 1691 the Jacobites were at Aughrim, blocking Ginkel's approach to Galway. Sarsfield suggested that the Jacobite army withdraw to Limerick, but St Ruth had the stronger position in higher ground, while the Williamites would have to cross a bog. However, the Williamites had twice as many heavy guns and Ginkel gave the order to attack on 12 July 1691, even though his men had just completed a long march.

The Jacobites appeared to be winning. However St Ruth was killed in the middle of the battle when he was decapitated by a cannonball, and this left the Jacobites in disarray. Most of them left the battlefield and retreated to Limerick.

DECAPITATED: had the head cut off

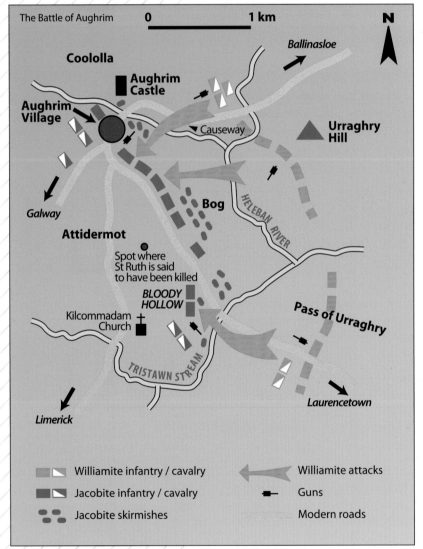

The Battle of Aughrim

0   1 km

N

- Ballinasloe
- Coololla
- Aughrim Castle
- Aughrim Village
- Causeway
- Urraghry Hill
- Galway
- Bog
- HELEBAN RIVER
- Attidermot
- Spot where St Ruth is said to have been killed
- BLOODY HOLLOW
- Kilcommadam Church
- Pass of Urraghry
- TRISTAWN STREAM
- Laurencetown
- Limerick

Legend:
- Williamite infantry / cavalry
- Jacobite infantry / cavalry
- Jacobite skirmishes
- Williamite attacks
- Guns
- Modern roads

THE TREATY OF LIMERICK

Ginkel followed the Jacobites to Limerick and it seemed as though there would be another long siege. However, the failure of French help to arrive and the sudden death of Tyrconnell persuaded other Jacobite leaders to agree to Ginkel's peace terms. Consequently, the Jacobites surrendered on 26 September 1691 and the **Treaty of Limerick** was signed in October 1691.

ARTICLES
Civil and Military,
Agreed upon the 3d. Day of *Octob.* 1691.
BETWEEN
The Right Honourable, Sir *Charles Porter*, Knight, and *Thomas Coningsby*, Efq; Lords Juftices of *Ireland*; and His Excellency the Baron *De Ginckle*, Lieutenant General, and Commander in Chief of the *Englifh* Army, *On the One Part*.
AND
The Right Honourable, *Patrick*, Earl of *Lucan*, Piercy Vifcount *Gallmoy*, Collonel *Nicholas Purcel*, Collonel *Nicholas Cufack*, Sir *Toby Butler*, Collonel *Garret Dillon*, and Collonel *John Brown*, *On the other Part*. In the Behalf of the *Irifh* Inhabitants, in the City and County of *Lymerick*, the Counties of *Clare*, *Kerry*, *Cork*, *Sligo*, and *Mayo*.

Extract from the Treaty of Limerick.

TPD

Q Why do you think the Williamites won at Aughrim?

The Treaty contained civil and military terms. Here are the most important ones:

Civil Terms

1. The property of Jacobite landowners who still held arms in Limerick would not be confiscated.
2. Irish Catholics were allowed to practise their religion.
3. Around 750,000 acres of land belonging to Catholics who had supported James were confiscated and given to William's supporters.
4. Ginkel was made Earl of Athlone and given 26,480 acres of land.

Military Terms

Irish Jacobite soldiers were offered three choices:

(a) They could return to their homes in peace.
(b) They could join the Williamite army and serve with it in Europe against France.
(c) They could go to France to fight for King James, in alliance with King Louis XIV, against William and his European allies.

If a soldier chose option (c) he would be given free transport to France, in English ships, with his wife and children.

Many Jacobite soldiers chose option (c), and at the end of 1691 almost 12,000 soldiers went to France in ships provided by Ginkel, or in French ships, which had arrived in Ireland just after the siege of Limerick.

These exiles are known as **The Wild Geese**, and they fought as the army of King James in Europe until 1697. After peace was restored in Europe many of them became part of the French army. Patrick Sarsfield was the most famous of these Wild Geese. He was killed in battle in 1693 in the Austrian Netherlands.

Do you think this was a fair treaty? Why or why not?

Mary died in 1694 and William in 1702. As they had no children, Mary's sister Anne became Queen. All her children had died so when she died in 1714, the nearest Protestant relative was the German George I. So began the **House of Hanover**. Not surprisingly, those who supported James II's second marriage felt his son, James Edward, should be King and there was an unsuccessful rebellion in 1715. Thirty years later, James II's grandson, **Bonnie Prince Charlie**, also tried unsuccessfully to gain the English throne.

ACTIVITY

Form into groups. Each group should research the life of one of the major figures mentioned in Units 31 – 34. Create a display on the classroom wall – or on another school notice board – about the life of the person you have chosen. Print out a picture of this person and put it in the centre of your display. In a circle round the picture, place facts about his or her life and career.

When all the displays are completed, spend some time looking at each display and discussing them.

Is there one of these people whom you would particularly like to meet? If so, what questions would you ask them?

UNIT 35: THE EIGHTEENTH CENTURY

An example of a cover of a Penal Law document

THE PENAL LAWS

This is the name given to a series of laws passed after 1691, mainly by the Irish Parliament. These laws had two main purposes:

(a) To exclude all those who remained Catholic from:

  (i) the right to carry arms (weapons)

  (ii) all professions except the medical

  (iii) political power at local and national level

  (iv) the possession of landed property except in a short-term leasehold basis

  (v) all education except that which endeavoured to convert them to Protestantism

  (vi) owning a horse worth more than £5

(b) By means of these laws, to encourage Irish Catholics, especially the landowning class, to convert to the Protestant religion.

Some Catholics did change their religion to avoid penalties, though most remained Catholic. Similar laws were applied in England, but as Catholics were in a minority there, these laws had only limited effect.

After 1728 Catholics were not allowed to vote at elections. If a son became a Protestant, he automatically became owner of his Catholic father's estate, even if his father was still alive.

Catholics were not the only religious group to suffer. Presbyterians discovered that they were also to be denied many rights. Their ministers could preach freely but could not perform marriage ceremonies. In 1704 Presbyterians were also banned from town councils and from holding other official positions.

 Q How did life for Catholics and Presbyterians in Ireland change as a result of the Penal Laws?

 ## ACTIVITY

Compare what you have learned about the Penal Laws with the terms of the Treaty of Limerick. Draw two columns in your notebook and in one column list the terms of the Treaty of Limerick. In the other column, list some of the Penal laws.

Some historians say that by implementing the Penal Laws, the Treaty of Limerick was torn up. Look at your two lists and write about 300 words, starting with: "In comparing the Treaty of Limerick with the Penal laws, I think..." Quote from both the Treaty terms and the Penal Laws to justify your opinion.

AMERICAN WAR OF INDEPENDENCE

In Unit 17 you learned how the English founded colonies on the east coast of North America. The colonies did very well, and by 1770 there were 2.6 million people living there, about a third of the population of Britain. Of these, around half a million were slaves who had been brought from Africa. The American colonies were divided into thirteen 'states', distributed along the east coast of America. The 'Seven Years War' with the French in 1756-63 resulted in England gaining control of the French colony of **Canada**.

As the American colonies became wealthier and more powerful, they began to resent the fact that they were ruled by the British without any say in the British government. Some Americans argued that the British had no right to make them pay taxes unless they were allowed such a role. A campaign began, under the slogan 'No Taxation Without Representation'. The British continued to impose taxes, and even imposed new laws which angered many Americans and made them determined to obtain self-rule. The British responded to the campaign for self-rule by sending an army to quell the rebellion, which resulted in the **American War of Independence**.

Led by **Thomas Jefferson**, the thirteen states issued the **Declaration of Independence** on 4 July 1776 and formed a republic which they called the **United States of America**.

QUELL: put down

American leaders preparing the Declaration of Independence in 1776. It was painted by John Trumbull in 1819.

ACTIVITY

Study this picture and answer these questions.

1. Do you think this could be an accurate representation of the occasion? Why or why not?
2. Comment on the flags on the wall.
3. What might the man at the table on the left be there for?
4. What adjectives would you use to describe the mood of this painting?
5. Who might all the people sitting on the chairs on the left be?
6. This painting shows people alive in 1776. The first successful European colony in America was at Jamestown, Virginia, in 1607. Allowing 30 years for one generation, work out what relation these descendants of the first settlers might be. For example, could the older men be grandsons? Great-great-grandsons?
7. Have you any other comments on the painting? If so, tell the class.

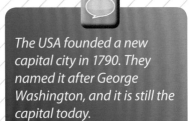

The USA founded a new capital city in 1790. They named it after George Washington, and it is still the capital today.

The British were determined not to lose control of their wealthy colonies, and fought a bitter war that lasted until 1781. The American army was led by **George Washington**, and was assisted by France, which provided weapons to the Americans. After a series of battles, the British finally conceded defeat after they were beaten at the Battle of Yorktown.

Why do you think the USA wanted to build a new capital city?

The USA was now an independent country, and in the course of the next century the young nation would extend its control all the way to the west coast of North America through a series of wars and treaties with the native Americans, the French, British, Spanish, Russians and Mexicans. By the mid 20th century it had become the wealthiest and most powerful country in the world. The British were shocked to have lost one of their most important colonies, but were soon trading profitably with the USA.

RESEARCH

Find out the names of the 13 states that declared independence and write them in a list.

Draw a coloured picture of their flag of 1776.

How many states are in the USA today? Write them out in a list.

Underline the most recent state to be added.

Underline the state that has the largest population today.

Look at the picture of the White House. If an historian needed to know what time of year this was taken, what evidence could he use? Could he make a good guess at the weather and the time of day? If so what features in the photograph would help him?

The White House in Washington, which contains the offices of the President of the USA. Work on this building began in 1792.

ACTIVITY

Take turns round the class to call out the name of a state in the United States today. Have someone write them down as they are chosen so that none are repeated. How long does it take to think of them all?

THE FRENCH REVOLUTION

From 1774 France was ruled by **King Louis XVI**. During his reign there was growing dissatisfaction within France. There were several reasons for this:

1. A series of bad harvests led to high food prices and malnutrition among the poor.
2. Very high taxes, especially on the poor.
3. Huge debts from fighting wars, most recently by helping the Americans against Britain.
4. The aristocrats in the government blocked attempts at reforming government, and were increasingly regarded as indifferent to the suffering of the poor.
5. The educated merchant classes had come to dislike the absolute rule of the King and wanted more equality and an end to the privileges given to noblemen and the church.

In May 1789 Louis called a meeting of people representing the three classes, or 'estates', of French society – the church, the nobility and the **'Third Estate'** – in order to find a solution to France's crippling debt. The Third Estate was anyone who was not nobility or clergy. Their representatives were mainly educated middle class people, but the Third Estate also included the common people. They eventually declared that they had the moral right to rule France because they represented 98% of French people. This is what one Frenchman wrote:

> *What is the Third Estate? Everything. What has it been until now in the political order? Nothing. What does it want to be? Something.*
>
> Abbé Sieyès, political theorist and Catholic clergyman, 1789

The King resisted their efforts, and once it became apparent that Louis was planning to use force against them, the people of Paris decided to capture a large store of ammunition in the **Bastille** prison in Paris. The prison had come to symbolise everything that was hated about the King and the nobility. This event, which took place on 14th July 1789, is called the **Storming of the Bastille** and this symbolic event marks the start of the **French Revolution**.

The leaders of the Revolution took away a lot of the King's power but, three years later, on 21st September 1792, there was a second revolution in which the King was deposed and imprisoned. The revolutionaries abolished the monarchy and declared France to be a republic.

The revolution soon worsened into a **reign of terror,** as the leaders used more and more violence against their opponents. Louis XVI was executed by guillotine on 21st January 1793 and his Queen, Marie Antoinette, was executed in October. Opposition to the Revolution was put down without mercy. Up to 40,000 people were executed without trial, by guillotine.

Alarmed by the prospect of the revolution spreading to other countries, nearby monarchs threatened France with war. This resulted in a conflict with Austria and Prussia from 1792, and Spain and Britain from 1793. The war was indecisive, and these countries eventually made peace with France (in Britain's case in 1802), and the revolution seemed secure.

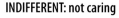

INDIFFERENT: not caring

Sometimes the media today are referred to as "The Fourth Estate"

DEPOSED: removed from a position of power

INDECISIVE: having no clear result

What is a guillotine? How did it work?

The major English poet, William Wordsworth, visited Paris during the Revolution in 1791 when he was 21 years old. He fell in love with a French woman called Annette Vallon and they had a daughter, Caroline. Wordsworth wanted to stay but his relatives were so worried about him that they stopped sending him money and he had to come home. He did not see his daughter for ten years, but in 1801 he visited Annette and Caroline. His sonnet, "It is a beauteous evening, calm and free", was written about a walk he took with his daughter on that visit.

This is what one French general wrote about his efforts to stamp out opposition in the region of Vendée in western France:

> *There is no more Vendée. It died with its wives and its children by our free sabres. ... According to the orders that you gave me, I crushed the children under the feet of the horses, massacred the women who, at least for these, will not give birth to any more brigands. I do not have a prisoner to reproach me. I have exterminated all.*

> General Francois Joseph Westermann, 1793 in a letter to the French government

ACTIVITY

You are an official in the Vendée who has survived General Westermann's massacre. You have seen his letter to the French government. You are so angry that you write a reply to him.

Word process your letter, formatting it as a modern letter. Describe your feelings about him and about what he did. Bring in your personal views on killing and any other moral or political position that you hold.

A painting of fighting in Vendée, painted by Jean Sorieul in 1852.

The terror ended by 1794, at which point weariness with war and violence led to a less extreme form of republican government. However the country was still crippled by debt and ravaged by years of war and in 1799 a military general, **Napoleon Bonaparte** took over the country and became dictator. This would eventually result in the **Napoleonic Wars**, characterised by a series of stunning victories over other European powers in the first part of the nineteenth century.

DICTATOR: a ruler who has absolute power

THE 1798 REBELLION IN IRELAND

In 1707 the Scottish Parliament had been abolished and Scotland and England had been united to form a single country, called the **United Kingdom of Great Britain**, with its Parliament in London. Ireland had its own Parliament, although it was still ruled by Britain.

In 1791 a group of Irishmen, inspired by the success of the revolutions in America and France, formed a society called the **United Irishmen**.

They were led by **Wolfe Tone** and were made up of all those groups oppressed by the Penal Laws, including Catholics and Presbyterians. They wanted more democracy and an end to religious oppression. A few of the laws were relaxed at this time, but the United Irishmen wanted more.

The French Revolutionary government sent an army of 14,000 troops to Ireland in 1796 to help the United Irishmen, but fierce storms prevented them from landing. Wolfe Tone said *"The English have had their luckiest escape since the Armada."*

Wolfe Tone, leader of the United Irishmen

 To what was Tone referring and what did he mean?

ACTIVITY

Read this comment from one writer about the United Irishmen:

"The organisation crossed the religious divide with a membership comprising Roman Catholics, Presbyterians, Methodists, other Protestant 'dissenters' groups, and some from the Protestant Ascendancy."

Share ideas on how so many different groups could come together to fight for one cause. What do you think is the key to such unity?

The British decided to stir up sectarianism in order to divide the rebels. The Lord Chancellor wrote:

> I have arranged... to increase the animosity between the Orangemen and the United Irishmen, or liberty men as they call themselves. Upon that animosity depends the safety of the centre counties of the North.

The British conducted a series of raids against the United Irishmen in 1798, and open rebellion broke out in May. The rebels rose up across Ireland, but after a ferocious conflict that lasted several months, they were finally defeated by the British.

The conflict was extremely bloody, with captured rebels and civilians alike killed in large numbers. It is estimated that around 10,000 people died in the conflict. Wolfe Tone was captured and committed suicide in prison in November 1798.

 How do you think the events of the American War of Independence and the French Revolution might have influenced the way the British reacted to the 1798 rebellion?

In response to the rebellion, the British decided to abolish the Irish Parliament and rule Ireland directly from the British Parliament and in 1800 the **Act of Union** was passed. This united Britain and Ireland under a single Parliament in London from the start of 1801. The country was then re-named the **United Kingdom of Great Britain and Ireland**.

Because the old Irish Parliament had been seen as corrupt and dominated by Protestants, the Catholic majority in Ireland initially supported the Union. However when it became clear that the London Parliament was not going to end the Penal Laws, they quickly turned against it. This led to a campaign for the Penal Laws to the lifted (**Catholic Emancipation**) and for a restoration of the Irish Parliament (**The Repeal Movement**).

These two issues would dominate Irish politics during the nineteenth century.

ACTIVITY

Choose *either* the American War of Independence, *or* the French Revolution *or* the 1798 Rebellion in Ireland. Summarise what happened, in your own words. Then write about how and why you think the event was significant. Write about 300 words in total.

ACTIVITY

Someone once said, "History is not a reason; it's an excuse."

Referring to some of the events you have studied in this Unit, can you work out what the speaker meant? Clue: think about events of the present day as well!

Review this Section

You may have had your own ideas on what happened during the years covered in the Units on Ireland in this Section. So many of the events are still talked about today. Have any of your views changed as a result of your studies?

How important is it to understand both sides in a situation in order to have a **valid** opinion on it? Explain your answer to this question.

You have read about three countries whose people rebelled against their rulers. Referring to the consequences of the rebellions you have studied, do you think it is all right to do this? If so, in what circumstances? If not, why not?

> **VALID: true, right**

Word Check

Check out these words to make sure you can spell them.

apprentice	siege	representation
Aughrim	artillery	concentrate
Limerick	dictator	assault
treason	Presbyterian	ammunition
dissenters	Methodist	Ginkel
garrison	alliance	decapitate
Sarsfield	animosity	

If you're not sure if you can spell any of them, check them out a few more times.

Class Quiz!

Divide into two teams and decide on a prize for the winning team. If you get a question right, your team gets a point, BUT if you get a question wrong, you lose a point! So think carefully before you answer.

1. Which country controlled Canada before 1763?

2. Fill in the blank: "In 1704 _____ were banned from town councils and from holding other official positions."

3. What was the date of the American Declaration of Independence?

4. What was the Earl of Tyrconnell's nickname?

5. Was Patrick Sarsfield a Williamite or a Jacobite?

6. Name two countries in The Grand Alliance.

7. What English poet visited Paris during the French revolution?

8. Who was Mary of Modena's husband?

9. In what year was the Siege of Derry?

10. What is the capital city of the United States of America and after whom is it named?

11. Who was the leader of the United Irishmen?

12. On 14th of July, the people of Paris stormed what?

13. In what year did the Act of Union between Britain and Ireland come into force?

14. Who was Louis XVI's wife?

15. Why is Robert Lundy reviled by some Protestants?

16. Who was the French king during the Williamite wars?

17. What is a mercenary?

18. Spell the name of the machine by which people were executed during the French revolution.

19. By how many days was the calendar adjusted in 1752?

20. What was the name of the ship that relieved the Siege of Derry?

KINGS AND QUEENS OF ENGLAND AND GREAT BRITAIN

1485–1509   Henry VII (son of Edmund Tudor)

1509–1547   Henry VIII (son of Henry VII)

1547–1553   Edward VI (son of Henry VIII)

1553–1558   Mary I (daughter of Henry VIII)

1558–1603   Elizabeth I (daughter of Henry VIII)

1603–1625   James I (son of Mary Queen of Scots)

1625–1649   Charles I (son James I)

1649   *The Commonwealth*

1649-1653   *Parliament (under military rule)*

1653–1658   Oliver Cromwell (Lord Protector)

1658–1659   Richard Cromwell (son of Oliver Cromwell)

1660   *Restoration*

1660–1685   Charles II (son of Charles I)

1685–1688   James II (son of Charles I)

Joint rule { **1688–1694**   Mary II (daughter of James II)

1688–1702   William III (William of Orange of the Netherlands)

1702–1707   Anne (daughter of James II)

1707   *Union of England and Scotland creates Kingdom of Great Britain*

1707-1714   Anne (continuation of reign before Union)

1714-1727   George I (son of the granddaughter of James VI)

1727-1760   George II (son of George I)

1760-1820   George III (grandson of George II)

COPYRIGHT NOTICES

INDEX